Judith—

Task Sonoma County!

Cheryl

John Hall

A Chefs

Playground!

down home : downtown

ISBN-13: 978-0-615-28546-7
ISBN-10: 0-615-28546-5

Manufactured and distributed by Favorite Recipes Press

**FRP.** INC

Favorite Recipes Press is an imprint of FRP, Inc.
a wholly owned subsidiary of Southwestern/Great American, Inc.
P.O. Box 305142, Nashville, Tennessee 37230
800-358-0560

Packaged and designed by Jennifer Barry Design, Fairfax, California
Project director: Robert Larsen
Copy editing by Carolyn Miller
Layout production by Kristen Hall
Recipe testing by Kate Washington

Printed in China
First Printing 2009

# down home : downtown

*Seasonal Recipes from Two Sonoma Wine Country Restaurants*

recipes by jeff mall and josh silvers

photographs by alan campbell
text by linda murphy

published by rodney strong vineyards

# contents

# down home recipes

## winter

Frisée Salad with Bacon and Deviled Eggs
Dungeness Crab–Stuffed Avocado with
   Mango and Red Chile Dressing

Zinfandel-Glazed Beef Short Ribs with
   Horseradish Mashed Potatoes and
   Bacon-Braised Brussels Sprouts
Lemon-Herb Roasted Chicken with
   Onion and Sage Cream Gravy, Braised
   Cabbage, and Biscuits

Meyer Lemon Cheesecake with Coconut
   Crust and Blood Orange Syrup
Chocolate and Peanut Butter Mousse
   Layer Cake

## spring

Spring Greens Salad with Bellwether
   Farms Pepato Cheese, Candied Pecans,
   and Pickled Onion
Grilled Gulf Shrimp Cocktail with Celery
   Salad and Zin Cocktail Sauce

Duck Breast "Pepper Steak" with Brandy
   and Green Peppercorns, Crispy Stone-
   Ground Grits, and Braised Greens with
   Apples and Bacon
Grilled Lamb Sirloin with Jalapeño-Mint
   Jelly, Grilled Asparagus, and Pecan
   Rice Pilaf

Butterscotch Crème Brûlée
Dark Chocolate Pound Cake with Jubilee
   Cherries

## summer

Tomato, Tomato, Tomato Salad
Chilled Melon Soup with Jalapeños
   and Mint

Bacon-Wrapped Wild King Salmon on
   Sweet Corn Grits with Roasted Tomato
   Broth and Arugula-Basil Salad
Grilled Rib-Eye "Ranchero," Summer
   Squash "Calabacitas," Grilled
   Scallions, and Warm Tortillas

Toasted Masa and Cornmeal Shortcakes
   with Fresh Berries and Crema
Warm Peach Turnovers with Vanilla Bean
   Ice Cream

## fall

Wild Mushroom and Goat Cheese Chile
   Rellenos with New Mexico Red Chile
   Sauce
Butternut Squash and Apple Soup with
   Lemon Cream and Crispy Sage

Apple Wood-Smoked Pork Chop with
   Fresh Applesauce, Braised Rainbow
   Chard, and Corn Bread Stuffing
New Orleans Red Bean "Cassoulet" with
   Crispy Duck, Ham Hock, and Andouille
   Sausage

Apple "Upside-Down" Cake with Salty
   Caramel and Whipped Cream
Southern Bread Pudding with Bourbon
   Sauce

# downtown recipes

## winter

Frisée Salad Lyonnaise
Josh's Crab Cakes with Sherry
    Mayonnaise

Braised Short Ribs with Horseradish
    Crème Fraîche, Mashed Potatoes, and
    Sautéed Spinach
Pan-Roasted Chicken Breast with
    Spaghetti Squash "Carbonara"

Mascarpone Cheesecake with Amarena
    Cherries
Chocolate Peanut Butter Pie with
    Chocolate Ice Cream

## spring

Syrah's Simple Mixed Greens with Goat
    Cheese for Spring Prawn Cocktail with
    Damn Good Cocktail Sauce

Pan-Roasted Sonoma Duck Breast with
    Mascarpone Polenta and Blackberry
    Gastrique
Grilled Lamb with Asparagus and Green
    Garlic Risotto

Butterscotch Pudding with Soft and
    Sexy Whipped Cream
Warm Chocolate Puddle Cakes with
    Cherry Cream

## summer

Heirloom Tomato Salad with Yellow
    Tomato Vinaigrette, Basil Oil, and
    Burrata Cheese
Spicy Watermelon Gazpacho

Grilled Wild King Salmon with Sweet Corn
    Panzanella
Grilled Rib-Eye Steak with Black Truffle
    Butter, Watercress Salad, and Salt-
    Roasted Potatoes

Mixed Berry Trifle with Meyer Lemon Curd
Grilled Peaches with Honey-Rosemary
    Sauce and Vanilla Ice Cream

## fall

Stuffed Poblano Chiles with Basmati Rice,
    Butternut Squash, and Cilantro Cream
Roasted Butternut Squash and Apple Soup

Pork Chops with Fennel-Apple Salad and
    Potato Pancakes
Deconstructed Cassoulet

Buttery Gravenstein Apple Cake with
    Mascarpone Sherbet
Whiskey Bread Pudding with Caramel
    Sauce

*"Sonoma County is a chef's playground. It's America's Provence. We grow and raise everything here!"* —Josh Silvers, Syrah

*I*n 1999, chefs Jeff Mall and Josh Silvers opened restaurants in Sonoma County, each drawn to that beautiful Northern California region by its diversity of culinary ingredients and wines.

"Like steel to a magnet" is how "Down Home" Jeff, a country boy who cooks hearty Southern- and Southwestern-inspired food, describes the pull Sonoma County had on him when he searched for a home for Zin Restaurant & Wine Bar, eventually finding it in Healdsburg. "The availability of terrific wines was a no-brainer, but the clincher was that I could have a house in the country and grow produce and raise chickens in my backyard."

"Sonoma County is a chef's playground," adds "Downtown" Josh, who opened his restaurant, Syrah Bistro, in Santa Rosa, the business and governmental hub of the county. A Berkeley-raised chef with a love of French and Italian cuisine, Josh combed California for a location for Syrah and was seduced by Sonoma County.

Many of the ingredients a restaurant chef and home cook could want are available in Sonoma, most of them locally grown or raised. Farm stands, farmers' markets, and gourmet grocers stock these ingredients, and some large, savvy supermarkets devote shelf and cooler space to Sonoma foods.

Zin and Syrah opened just three months apart, at a time when Sonomans hungered for new flavors and more dining choices. As with most other wine regions of the world, Sonoma's culinary scene began to broaden once its wines earned acclaim, and Jeff and Josh were among the first out-of-town chefs to relocate, having recognized the quality of the Sonoma County food products available to them.

Santa Rosa, a bustling city of 160,000 residents, was ready for a restaurant committed to using super-fresh local ingredients and serving elegant European-influenced dishes. With Syrah, it got that and much more: four- and seven-course tasting menus, wine pairings, a wine list boasting 250 selections, and a retail wine shop. Its location in the historic Railroad Square section of downtown added a sophisticated dining option to "restaurant row" and its dozen eateries.

Healdsburg, once a sleepy village of farmers, ranchers, and winemakers, has blossomed into a lively tourism center, with restaurants, hotels, winery tasting rooms, and easy access to the wineries in the Alexander, Dry Creek, and Russian River valleys. Before Jeff came to town, Healdsburgers frequently drove to Santa Rosa to dine out. Once they tried his boldly flavored dishes, featuring produce and eggs he grows and raises himself, and the array of Zinfandel wines on the list, they had a reason to stay home. The success of Zin opened the door to other restaurateurs to set up shop in Healdsburg.

Before Zin and Syrah, Sonoma County had no Grilled Certified Angus Hanger Steak with Rancho Beans or Wild Mushroom and Goat Cheese Chile Rellenos with New Mexico Red Chile Sauce (Jeff), or the rich, chunky crab cakes Josh serves in a number of ways: with arugula and potato salad with béarnaise dressing and salsa verde one day, with sherry mayonnaise the next.

Sonoma County is an hour's drive north of San Francisco, bounded by the Pacific Ocean on the west and the Mayacamas Mountains on the east. With its rainy yet moderate winters, brilliant springtime sun, and warm summer and fall days cooled at night by Pacific Ocean breezes and fog, the region is perfect for growing wine grapes and just about anything else a chef could want.

Jeff and Josh were early embracers of this agricultural treasure trove, and other chefs followed, transforming Sonoma into wine and food country. The raw ingredients had been there all along, first discovered in the 1970s by forward-looking, socially conscious chefs such as Alice Waters of Chez Panisse restaurant in Berkeley, who fueled the Bay Area culinary revolution.

9

Yet it took until the late 1990s for the menus of Sonoma County restaurants to truly reflect the region's bounty: seafood from the coast, lamb, poultry, cheeses, olive oils, vinegars, honey, eggs, artisan breads, and a cornucopia of produce, including apples, pears, stone fruits, berries, melons, citrus, heirloom tomatoes, lettuces, squashes, eggplant, root vegetables, peppers, and fresh herbs.

More and more of these foods are grown organically and sustainably by farmers who eschew chemical fertilizers and herbicides, by ranchers who treat their animals humanely, and by fishermen who use lines instead of nets and understand that they must limit their catches now, so that seafood will continue to thrive in the future.

Today, growers deliver their just-picked fruits, vegetables, and fresh herbs to the back doors of area restaurants and grocery stores. Most Sonoma County towns and cities have farmers' markets. Sonoma food products are so sought after by city slickers that farmers and ranchers travel to San Francisco regularly to sell their specialties at the Ferry Plaza Farmers Market and to restaurants and high-end grocers. Nearly as many visitors to Sonoma County taste their way along the Sonoma County Farm Trails route as they do the wine roads.

Even Napa Valley, one of America's most recognized dining meccas, sources fish, meats, produce, and condiments from Sonoma County, its neighbor to the west.

The inspiration for this book was a summer evening in 2008, at the home of Rodney Strong Vineyards owner Tom Klein, in Sonoma County's Alexander Valley. Tom, whose winery has produced wine for more than fifty years, knew that Jeff and Josh occasionally cooked at events as a team, and asked them to prepare a five-course dinner for forty people in conjunction with the Sonoma Wine Country Weekend celebration.

In Iron Chef fashion, Jeff and Josh took the same main ingredients and applied their own accents—Mall's Southern comfort versus Silvers's classic, refined style. The chefs' dishes were served side by side, so diners could compare two preparations of the same main ingredient. While no formal vote was taken, it was agreed that the Sonoma County chefs ended in a tie. Both chefs won.

For example, Jeff's Bacon-Wrapped Wild King Salmon on Sweet Corn Grits with Roasted Tomato Broth and Arugula-Basil Salad offered deep, savory flavors—a complex and substantial dish. Josh's Grilled Wild King Salmon with Sweet Corn Panzanella was more delicate yet equally flavorful, with the naturally fatty richness of the salmon offset by the sweet summer corn and tangy aioli.

For dessert, Jeff made a baked peach turnover, spiced with cinnamon and nutmeg and served with vanilla bean ice cream. Josh seasoned peaches with honey and rosemary, grilled them until their sugars concentrated and their flesh turned soft, then topped them with vanilla ice cream and fresh raspberries. Same fruit, but two very different desserts.

Go behind the scenes, and the Jeff-and-Josh contrast is even more profound: Jeff drives a 1964 boxwood green/Wimbledon white Ford pickup truck, which lacks power steering and air conditioning. Josh drives a steel-blue metallic Honda Ridgeline truck equipped with four-wheel drive and GPS.

Jeff carries his knives in a red toolbox; Josh's blades arrive in a wheeled black suitcase. For the Rodney Strong dinner, Jeff prepped and grilled outside, Josh cooked inside. Jeff grows his own produce and raises chickens for their eggs at his Eastside Farm in the Russian River Valley, a few miles southwest of Healdsburg; Josh purchases fresh ingredients from local purveyors, including tomatoes from Healdsburg's Dan Magnuson of Soda Rock Farm and chiles from Tierra Vegetables.

Jeff bakes his own hamburger buns; Josh purchases his breads from Della Fattoria Bakery in Petaluma, a purveyor beloved by Bay Area chefs and known for its dense, complex loaves and rounds, many of them flavored with fruits and herbs.

Zin is informal, with bare tabletops and standard flatware. Food servers are clad in blue jeans and white shirts, fitting Jeff's farm theme. A blue-plate special is featured every night, and the wine bar is a favorite hangout for local vintners.

Syrah has multicourse tasting menus with wine pairings, thirteen artisanal cheeses from which diners can design their own course, and Petite Syrah, a retail wine shop. Tablecloths, fine stemware, and flatware specific to each course are set at Syrah's tables; servers wear smart black shirts and slacks.

Jeff and his wife, Susan, ate their way through Louisiana and Mississippi, en route to a Southern Foodways Alliance Symposium in Oxford, Mississippi, where chefs devoted to preserving traditional Southern foods and recipes gather. Josh and his wife, Regina, co-owner of Syrah Bistro, traveled to Turin, Italy, in a similar search for culinary inspiration, in conjunction with Josh's role as Sonoma County's chef delegate to the Slow Foods International convivium, Terra Madre.

Yet for all their differences, Jeff and Josh are great friends and cook together often. They donate food and their time to several Sonoma County charitable groups; assist the Worth Our Weight program, which provides culinary, organic farming and business management training to disadvantaged young people in

Sonoma County; and support Slow Food, the movement that promotes the raising and consumption of sustainably raised local foods.

Neither chef uses trendy culinary techniques, such as cooking sous-vide ("under vacuum") or molecular gastronomy (chemistry in the kitchen). Instead, their dishes evolve from their devotion to local products and the freshest, in-season ingredients, and from their desire to let the pure, natural flavors of the ingredients speak for themselves.

Jeff and Josh share the belief that there is no better place in America to eat than in Sonoma County. The recipes in this book reflect their view, although cooks outside Sonoma can duplicate many of the recipes by substituting local ingredients that are similar.

"The important thing for home cooks is to use fresh ingredients that are at the peak of season," Josh says. "If local tomatoes aren't in season, you won't find tomatoes in our dishes. I change the menu as the seasons change, so that only the best-tasting ingredients make it to the plate."

Adds Jeff: "When the summer season ends and the farmers' markets take a winter break, we still have access to fresh, local ingredients, including mushrooms, Meyer lemons, chestnuts, squashes, and winter greens. That's why Josh and I change our menus, to take advantage of the variety of products that become available throughout the year."

*Down Home : Downtown* captures the flavor and seasonality of Sonoma County through the contrasting culinary styles of Jeff Mall and Josh Silvers. Inspired by their head-to-head "battle" at the Rodney Strong Vineyards dinner, this cookbook pairs each chef's recipe for the same Sonoma-grown main ingredient on facing pages.

Jeff's Southern leanings are obvious in his New Orleans Red Bean "Cassoulet" with Crispy Duck, Ham Hock, and Andouille Sausage, while on the opposite page you'll find Josh's Deconstructed Cassoulet recipe, which transports diners to southwestern France, with traditional meats and white beans making for a more classic, yet also contemporary, rendition.

The counterpoints in *Down Home : Downtown* are many, yet Jeff Mall and Josh Silvers are on common ground when it comes to their passion for Sonoma County's dynamic ingredients and superb wines.

down home

downtown

"The dishes at Zin are Americana, enhanced variations on the theme of Southern comfort food. As the son of a California farmer, I grew up eating fresh farm produce and locally raised meats, which is what I bring to the restaurant, with some wine country twists and tweaks." —Jeff Mall, Zin

# ZIN down home

Until partners Jeff Mall and Scott Silva opened Zin Restaurant & Wine Bar in May 1999, Healdsburg had limited dining choices. Only mom-and-pop delicatessens, a few Asian eateries, taquerias, and a couple of fine-dining establishments existed then, so Zin was welcomed for its American South/ Southwestern cuisine, casual atmosphere, and a wine list focused on Zinfandel and other flavorful Sonoma County wines.

Located one block north of Healdsburg's historic plaza, Zin quickly became a hangout for local farmers in Wranglers, winemakers in polar fleece vests, and visitors in designer jeans, all drawn by Jeff's "down home" dishes and Scott's wine list.

"Healdsburg was an obvious location for the restaurant, not only for the local ingredients available to us, but for the bold, complex wines produced by our neighbors, which go so well with hearty food like ours," Jeff says.

The Zin vibe is casual, the pace unhurried. Contemporary paintings of farm scenes hang on the exposed walls, and behind the bar is a wall of wine stored in wooden racks that rise to the high ceiling. A skylight brightens the room by day, and at night, soft lighting gives the room an amber glow.

Diners can belly up to the open kitchen to watch Jeff as he cooks. Food is served on simple, white ceramic plates, and there are no tablecloths to fuss with, although cloth napkins are most welcome when tucking into the St. Louis-style ribs.

In his dishes, Jeff makes optimum use of Sonoma County ingredients, many of which he and his wife, Susan Dunphy Mall, grow organically on their Eastside Farm, and on leased farmland in nearby Windsor.

"When we opened Zin, we used the very best products our local growers and farmers' markets could provide," Jeff explains. "This eventually led us to plant our own garden to supply the restaurant. We grow our own beans, squash, peppers, herbs, and heirloom tomatoes, and our fruit trees and berry bushes provide us with apples, pears, plums, nectarines, strawberries, and blackberries."

"Chicken Mama" Susan raises forty chickens, which lay the eggs Jeff uses in his dishes. He makes his own sausage, cures his own bacon, and uses a New Mexico–style roaster to turn his home-grown chiles into deeply flavored, spicy (but not super-hot) additions to his cooking.

Jeff takes great pride in the dozens of varieties of heirloom tomatoes he and Susan grow. Every spring, Jeff begins with a thousand seed starts in the basement of his home, giving them light, water, and

TLC until it's time to plant the starts in the garden. Approximately five hundred go into the ground, with the remaining five hundred being loaded onto Jeff's pickup and taken to Zin for the "big free tomato giveaway." Anyone can grab a couple of plants, though they won't know what variety they have until the tomatoes begin to ripen. "I tell people, 'Plant them and see what you get,'" Jeff says. "When the tomatoes become ripe, some folks bring them to the restaurant so I can help them identify the type."

Jeff is known for his blue plate specials, which draw regulars who come in for his St. Louis–Style Ribs in Zin Barbecue Sauce, Yankee Pot Roast, Buttermilk Fried Chicken, and other specialties. Although his training was at the prestigious Culinary Institute of America in Hyde Park, New York, and he has worked with such acclaimed chefs as Jeremiah Tower, Mark Franz, and Bradley Ogden, Southern-style food, made with local ingredients, was Jeff's passion. Zin's menu includes braised short ribs, Mexican beer-battered green beans with mango salsa, deviled eggs, sweet corn grits, and flaky baking powder biscuits.

"The late winemaker Rodney Strong once said that Zin's food was like mother's milk," Jeff recalls. "Our dishes are simple variations on the theme of comfort food, with wine country enhancements."

## JEFF'S PANTRY LIST

One of the tomatoes Jeff cultivates is the Italian San Marzano variety, which he cans for use during the winter and spring months. He also makes his own catsup, barbecue dry rub, hot pepper jelly, and Zinfandel jelly for the restaurant, with most of the ingredients coming from his garden.

**On the Shelf**
Chipotle chiles in adobo sauce
Condiments
   Gulden's Spicy Brown Mustard, Mae Ploy
   Sweet Chilli Sauce, Nana Mae's Organics
   apple cider vinegar, Sriracha hot sauce,
   Tabasco sauce, Zin's house-made catsup
   (page 64)
Dried Mexican chiles
Grains
   Falls Mill stone-ground grits, masa harina,
   Ridgecut Gristmills stone-ground
   cornmeal
Hector's Honey
Kosher salt
Nuts
   almonds, pecans, walnuts
Oil
   canola oil, extra-virgin olive oil
Pickled jalapeños en escabeche
Potatoes
Raisins
Spirits
   brandy, dry sherry
Zin's canned San Marzano tomatoes
Zin's house-made barbecue dry rub (page 128)
Zin's house-made hot pepper jelly

**In the Fridge**
Dairy
   Clover Stornetta milk, Laura Chenel goat
   cheese, Parmigiano-Reggiano cheese, Zin's
   house-made ricotta cheese
Eastside Farm eggs
House-made dill pickles
Meat
   ham hocks, Zin's house-made bacon
   (or high-quality purchased bacon),
   Zoe's Meats prosciutto
Produce
   cabbage, Gourmet Mushrooms, limes,
   romaine lettuce

*"Our dishes are inspired by French and Italian cooking,
yet rely on the awesome Sonoma County ingredients available to us
year-round. Syrah Bistro's food is elegant and presented with style,
yet not pretentious or fussy."* —Josh Silvers, Syrah

## SYRAH **downtown**

Josh Silvers lives and works in Santa Rosa, Sonoma County's largest city, and doesn't have the luxury of a produce garden, a chile roaster, or a henhouse in his backyard. Yet he has a bounty of farm- and ocean-fresh Sonoma County ingredients at his fingertips: wild Pacific salmon, Liberty Duck from Sonoma County Poultry, chiles and other vegetables from Tierra Vegetables in Windsor, apple cider vinegar from Nana Mae's Organics in Sebastopol, and dozens of other locally grown products. Though he's without a farm, the farmers come to him.

Josh is decidedly downtown, in both the location of his restaurant (in Santa Rosa's Railroad Square district) and his Paris-meets-Florence style of cooking. He's a big fan of Laura Chenel goat cheese from Sonoma, which

he discovered while dining at Alice Waters's renowned Chez Panisse restaurant in Berkeley, his hometown. He buys tomatoes from Soda Rock Farm in Alexander Valley, whose owner, Dan Magnuson, annually battles Jeff for the title of best heirloom tomato grower in Sonoma County. Josh's acclaimed crab cakes are made from Dungeness crabs caught off the Sonoma Coast, and his cheesecakes get their richness from mascarpone cheese produced by Clover Stornetta Farms in Petaluma.

"The restaurant's name comes from the cemented relationship of wine and food— the fact that we are in world-class wine country, with amazing local ingredients in our backyard," Josh says. "Take Della Fattoria. The Weber family has an incredible passion for bread and makes the most amazing boules (rounds) from their wood-burning oven. People come up to me at Syrah all the time to say how much they like the bread. We pay more for this level of quality, but it's worth it."

Josh is most proud of his seven-course tasting menu, which typically starts with soup and moves on to a fish course, then dishes showcasing duck, lamb, pork, beef, finishing with either a cheese or a dessert course. For an additional cost, he'll pour the perfect glass of wine with each dish, the flavor and texture either complementing or contrasting the food. The seasonal menu changes every month and on Josh's whim.

The wine list, 250 bottles strong, is built around Syrah, of course (there are fifty on the list), plus a wealth of other choices: Sauvignon Blanc, Chardonnay, Pinot Noir, Cabernet Sauvignon, Merlot, Zinfandel, eight sparkling wines, and a sprinkling of international bottles. All the wines, including small-production Syrahs and Pinot Noirs that are difficult to find in stores, can be purchased at retail prices in Petite Syrah, the cozy wine shop adjacent to the restaurant.

Josh and Regina Silvers opened Syrah Bistro in 1999, three months ahead of the launch of Zin Restaurant & Wine Bar. Josh had worked his way up through several Bay Area restaurants, with his most powerful inspiration coming from Cindy Pawlcyn, his mentor at Mustards Grill in Napa Valley, and his father, kitchen designer and chef Don Silvers.

"I was cooking at an Orinda restaurant and wondering how I could transfer my passion into my own place," Josh recalls. "Regina said, 'I'll find the money and you find the place.'

I knew I wanted a high-end restaurant in Sonoma County, urban and elegant, and together, we made it happen."

The interior of Syrah is industrial-chic, a juxta-position of cement floors and an open, timbered ceiling, with eclectic artwork by Josh's mother, Monica Maass, and local artists. An atrium dining area adjacent to the main room is bright and airy.

Just as Jeff and Susan Mall work as a team, so do Josh and Regina; she handles the business side of Syrah Bistro while caring for their young son, Jackson; Josh mans the stoves, working with a staff that for the most part has been with him since opening day.

The Silvers and Malls are friends and huge fans of each other's cuisine, and they frequently work together on charitable causes. "In Sonoma County, all the chefs are friends and like to cook together," Josh says. "There is a symbiotic relationship in Sonoma County between wineries, chefs, and food people that's very exciting. We all hit the farmers' market for fresh ingredients and not the supermarket. The produce is fresher, it tastes better, and we appreciate knowing where our food is grown and the people who grew it."

The Silvers opened Jackson's Bar & Oven, named after their son, in the fall of 2009. It's a stone's throw from Syrah, with a full bar and a menu to include pizzas, pastas, burgers, salads, and buckets of chicken wings. The centerpiece is a wood-fired pizza oven, something Josh had long admired in Jeff's backyard. Even a downtown guy can have a little down home in him.

## JOSH'S PANTRY LIST

Many of Josh's ingredients come from local farms, ranches, and food purveyors. His cooking reflects both French and Italian influences, so his pantry list is longer than Jeff's, yet his dishes still shout "Sonoma."

### On the Shelf
Apple juice
Beans
    baby butter, black, black beluga lentils, cannellini, marrow
Dried fruit
    cherries, currants, golden raisins
Fregola and orzo pasta
Herbs and spices
    Allspice, anise seeds, bay leaf, black pepper, caraway seeds, cayenne pepper, celery seeds, chile powder, Chinese five-spice powder, cinnamon, cloves, coriander, cumin, dry mustard, oregano, pickling spice, poppy seeds, red pepper flakes, star anise, Szechuan peppercorns, turmeric, white pepper
Israeli couscous
Marshall's Farm Sonoma wildflower honey
Nuts
    almonds, candied pistachios, pine nuts, walnuts
Oils
    DaVero extra-virgin olive oil, DaVero Meyer lemon oil, truffle oil
Panko (Japanese bread crumbs)
Polenta
Pomegranate molasses
Porcini mushroom powder

Rice
    Black Foreboder wild rice, Lundberg jasmine and basmati
Salt
    Hawaiian red, Himalayan pink, kosher, Maldon, smoked kosher
Scharffen Berger chocolate
    cocoa nibs and cocoa powder
Sriracha chile sauce
Tabasco sauce
Terra Sonoma verjus
Tierra Vegetables chiles
    ancho, guajillo, New Mexico
Vin cotto
    (non-alcoholic, unfermented grape juice)
Vinegars
    DaVero red wine vinegar, Nana Mae's Organics apple cider vinegar, Sparrow Lane Champagne and Zinfandel vinegars

### In the Fridge
Best Foods mayonnaise
Cage-free eggs
Cured meats
    La Quercia coppa, prosciutto di Parma
Dairy
    Clover Stornetta milk, cream, and mascarpone cheese
Edmond Fallot Dijon and grain mustards
Yuzu citrus juice

"*Just as Jeff Mall and Josh Silvers focus on local ingredients for their dishes, Rodney Strong Vineyards has relied on Sonoma County grapes for our wines for fifty years. Our vineyards are sustainably farmed and are among the best in Sonoma County. We continue to look for new ways to capture the essence of the region in the bottle.*" —Tom Klein, proprietor

# rodney strong

23

The vision of Rodney Strong Vineyards is the same as that of Zin Restaurant & Wine Bar and Syrah Bistro: to harvest Sonoma County's bounty to produce products that use only the highest-quality ingredients. *Down Home:Downtown* came together after Jeff and Josh cooked at several Rodney Strong Vineyards events and discovered that the winery shared their passion for eating and drinking locally.

Rodney Strong winemaker Rick Sayre says, "My job is much like that of a chef; the best-quality raw ingredients make for the best wine. That's why we grow our own grapes, in addition to working with dedicated longtime Sonoma County Growers."

Former Paris and Broadway dancer Rodney Strong started making wine in 1959 and ultimately chose Sonoma County as home for Rodney Strong Vineyards. Until his death in 2006, Rod was to Sonoma County what Robert Mondavi was to Napa Valley: a winemaking and viticultural pioneer, industry leader, and inspirational advocate to Americans for enjoying wine with their meals on an everyday basis, not just on special occasions.

Tom Klein, a fourth-generation California farmer and a successful businessman, purchased the Healdsburg winery and associated vineyards with his family in 1989. He and Rick Sayre added new vineyards, replanted existing plots to specialized rootstocks and grape clones, and created a "winery within a winery," in which small lots of the highest-quality grapes get extra attention for the reserve

and single-vineyard bottlings. Rodney Strong Merlot and Cabernet Sauvignon wines come from the warm Alexander Valley. Cool-climate-loving Sauvignon Blanc, Chardonnay, and Pinot Noir are grown in the Russian River Valley. Old-vine estate vineyards yield the grapes for Rodney Strong's Knotty Vine Zinfandel, California's signature varietal and namesake of Jeff's restaurant. Rodney Strong's Alexander Valley Syrah suits Josh Silvers's Syrah Bistro menu to a T.

The climate during the Sonoma County growing season (warm days moderated at night by Pacific Ocean breezes and fog) and myriad soil types combine to give the county a diversity of wine styles unsurpassed by any other region in the United States. Expert viticulture and winemaking techniques further enhance the quality of the wines, and the pairing of food to wine is an ongoing pleasure.

There are no set-in-stone rules for matching wine and food (and vice versa), and everyone's taste is different. There are some basic pairing guidelines, though it's fine to simply drink the wines you like with the foods you like. Rarely are there truly bad matches, though some are certainly more harmonious than others. Experimentation is part of the fun.

Some pairings are tried-and-true winners: earthy Pinot Noir with duck and mushroom dishes; crisp, gently herbaceous Sauvignon Blanc with salads, shellfish, and fresh goat cheese; savory Merlot with rosemary-spiked lamb; muscular Cabernet Sauvignon with a medium-rare beef steak.

## Basic Wine-Pairing Principles

• Balanced wines—those with fruitiness, acidity, tannins, oak notes, and alcohol all in equal measure, so that no one component stands out— are winners with most foods.

• Match delicate wines with delicate dishes, and hearty wines with hearty foods. Light-bodied Pinot Gris, Sauvignon Blanc, and brut sparkling wine are ideal for a chilled shrimp or crab salad, yet a medium-bodied red wine, such as Pinot Noir, would be a better match for a salad topped with Asian-spiced, seared ahi tuna.

• High-acid foods such as vinaigrettes, tomatoes, olives, and citrus-flavored dishes call for high-acid white wines, such as Sauvignon Blanc, Riesling, and dry sparkling wine. If serving a red, make sure it has high natural acidity, such as Sangiovese, to compete with the acid in the dish.

• Contrast dishes that are rich (lobster), creamy (cream sauces), or have a high fat content (cheese) with high-acid white wines (Sauvignon Blanc, sparkling wine), which cut through the richness.

• Alternately, serve rich dishes with rich, fleshy wines: Chardonnay and Viognier, for example.

• High-protein red meats such as steaks, roasts, and leg of lamb benefit from service with red wines that have a significant tannin structure to cut through the fat in the meat. Cabernet Sauvignon, Merlot, and Bordeaux-style red blends do the trick.

• Spicy flavors call for bold, spicy wines. A classic match is barbecued beef or pork ribs with Zinfandel.

• Peppers and hot spices such as chili powder, peppercorns, and cayenne pepper are best tamed by moderate-alcohol wines (12.5 percent by volume or less), such as rosé and White Zinfandel, semi-dry whites, including Riesling and Gewürztraminer.

• Serve fruity wines with fruit-based dishes— Sauvignon Blanc with lemon chicken, Riesling with dishes featuring peaches and apricots, and Pinot Noir and Syrah for berry sauces.

• For desserts, select wines that are as sweet as the dish. If the dessert is sweeter than the wine, the wine becomes lost in the mouth; a wine that's sweeter than the dish overwhelms the dessert. Try late-harvest wine styles, including Riesling, Chardonnay, and Viognier, and for chocolate desserts, late-harvest Zinfandels and port-style, fortified red wines.

**Pork and veal:** Gewürztraminer, Chardonnay, Riesling, Pinot Noir

**Ham:** Chardonnay, Riesling, Pinot Noir

**Poultry:** Sauvignon Blanc, Chardonnay, Pinot Noir, Merlot, Syrah, dry rosé

**Tomato sauces:** Barbera, Sangiovese, Tempranillo

**Fruit-based desserts:** Late-harvest Riesling and Gewürztraminer, Muscat

**Chocolate desserts:** Late-harvest and port-style red wines

## Wine Storage Tips

• Store at cool temperatures. For short-term aging, keep bottles at temperatures under 70°F; for longer-term aging, 55° to 57°F is ideal.

• Cooler temperatures will slow the development of wine in the bottle; temperatures above 70°F degrees can "cook" the wine, depriving it of its vibrancy and longevity. Wines that get too warm expand in the bottle, pushing the cork out or causing wine to leak through cracks in the cork, exposing the wine to unwanted oxidation.

• Don't leave wine in the trunk of a car, above a refrigerator or oven, or under cool-white fluorescent lighting.

• Corks need to remain moist in order to maintain a firm seal and prevent oxidation, so store bottles on their sides or upside down to keep the liquid in contact with the cork.

• For most California wines, dry whites should be enjoyed within one to four years of the vintage date, when they are still fresh and lively. Most red wines can be aged three to seven years from the vintage date, although some full-bodied, tannic reds, such as Cabernet Sauvignon and Cabernet-based blends, can last longer.

## Wine Serving Tips

• Serve white wines slightly chilled; pull them from the refrigerator about 20 minutes before you're ready to pour. Wines that are too cold smell and taste dull and lack fruitiness.

• Serve red wines a few degrees colder than room temperature. If the bottle feels warm or room temperature to the touch, put it in the refrigerator for 15 minutes or an ice bucket for 5 minutes before opening.

• Some wines, particularly tannic red wines, benefit from aeration, so pour them into a decanter 30 minutes before serving.

• One standard, 750-ml wine bottle yields 24 ounces, or six 4-ounce glasses. For a dinner party, count on each guest drinking two to three 4-ounce glasses of wine. Some will consume more, some less.

• Depending on the menu and the wine preferences of guests, it's best to serve both white and red wines with a meal, with perhaps a sparkling wine or dry rosé to serve as an aperitif, making it available at dinner as well. Many people drink "only white" or "only red," so accommodate both groups, even if you know that Sauvignon Blanc is probably not the best match with the leg of lamb on the menu.

• Leftover wine, both white and red, can be resealed and stored in the refrigerator for up to 3 days.

## Common Pairings

**Salty snacks:** Sauvignon Blanc, brut sparkling wine

**Salads and vegetables:** Sauvignon Blanc, Riesling

**Mild cheeses:** Sauvignon Blanc, Chardonnay, Pinot Noir, Merlot, Cabernet Sauvignon

**Strong cheeses:** Chardonnay, Pinot Noir, Merlot, Cabernet Sauvignon, Syrah, Zinfandel

**Shellfish:** Sauvignon Blanc, Chardonnay, Chenin Blanc, dry sparkling wine

**Salmon and tuna:** Chardonnay, Pinot Noir

**Seafood with light sauces:** Sauvignon Blanc, Chardonnay, Viognier, dry sparkling wine

**Seafood with rich cream sauces:** Chardonnay, Viognier, dry sparkling wine

**Pasta with meat sauce:** Pinot Noir, Merlot, Cabernet Sauvignon, Sangiovese

**Asian dishes:** Sauvignon Blanc, Riesling, Gewürztraminer, Zinfandel, dry rosé

**Beef and barbecue-sauced meats:** Merlot, Cabernet Sauvignon, Syrah, Zinfandel

**Duck:** Pinot Noir, Syrah

**Game birds:** Pinot Noir, Merlot, Cabernet Sauvignon, Syrah, Zinfandel

**Lamb:** Pinot Noir, Merlot, Cabernet Sauvignon, Syrah, Zinfandel

# winter

*Grapevines go into dormancy, shedding their leaves for a three-month hibernation. Rainstorms give the sleeping vines and fruit trees the deep drink they'll need when they wake up in spring. Cold gray fog saturates the land, while root vegetables, Meyer lemons, and Dungeness crab lend life to the winter table.*

Chilly temperatures, fog, and plentiful rain mark the Sonoma wine country winter. The rains fill lakes and streams with precious water to be used for drinking and summer irrigation, to help sustain fish habitats, and to give the roots of dormant grapevines and trees a big gulp before it's time to blossom. Workers meticulously prune the vineyards so that vines will push out tender green buds in spring and begin to form clusters. Winter is high season for mushroom foragers, and Meyer lemon lovers are in heaven. Late-maturing apple varieties yield their crunchy fruit through December, and local chestnuts do indeed roast over open fires. Soul-warming dishes come from the Zin and Syrah kitchens: slow-braised meats; roasted poultry; squash soups and side dishes; winter greens such as kale, frisée, curly endive, and mustard, whose flowers form a canary-yellow carpet between vine rows early in the year. Yet the most anticipated winter ingredient just might be Sonoma Coast Dungeness crab, which is at its meatiest and most succulent from Thanksgiving through January.

## FRISÉE SALAD WITH BACON AND DEVILED EGGS

*This salad is my version of the classic salade lyonnnaise. It's a down-home version using good bacon and deviled eggs. At Zin, we cure and smoke our own bacon and gather eggs from our own flock of hens. You don't have to go through such trouble, though; just seek out top-quality bacon and local fresh eggs.*

*This classic French bistro salad is similar to Jeff's, in that we both use good-quality smoked bacon and farm-fresh eggs. Unlike Jeff, I don't have my own chickens and smoker in my backyard. Fortunately, I can buy great bacon and eggs from local farmers. The poached egg, when broken, enriches all the ingredients in the dish.*

**HOBBS' APPLEWOOD SMOKED BACON**

*Hobbs Shore, born Huna Schadden, came to the United States from Romania in the early 1930s and learned how to smoke meat from his grandparents, using coals and apple-wood chips. Seeing it as a chore, Hobbs abandoned the craft and, after several careers, retired to Marshall in West Marin County, California, where he resumed meat-smoking as a hobby. As the story goes, Hobbs delivered his smoked bacon to a party attended by Bay Area chefs, who were wowed by its taste. Soon Hobbs' Applewood Smoked Meat Company was a thriving, word-of-mouth business, and today, it sells predominantly to restaurants and a handful of Bay Area gourmet grocers. Hobbs died in 2008, at age eighty-six, yet his legendary dry-brined and smoked bacon, and other smoked meats, remain on chefs' must-have lists.*

**Deviled Eggs**
6 large eggs
¼ cup mayonnaise
1 ½ pickled jalapeño chiles, minced
2 teaspoons pickled jalapeño juice from can
2 teaspoons minced fresh chives, plus more
   for garnish
Kosher salt and freshly ground pepper
   to taste

**Frisée Salad**
2 heads frisée or curly endive, outer leaves
   discarded
8 slices bacon, cut into small dice
1 shallot, minced
1 teaspoon Dijon mustard
¼ cup sherry vinegar
¼ cup canola oil
Kosher salt and freshly ground pepper
   to taste

For the deviled eggs: Put the eggs in a deep saucepan and add water to cover. Place over high heat, bring to a boil, and boil for 1 minute. Remove from the heat, cover, and let stand for 10 minutes. Drain the water, roll the eggs gently around inside the pan to crack the shells, and place in a bowl of ice water for 15 minutes. Peel the eggs and cut them in half lengthwise. Push the yolks through a sieve into a small bowl and mix with the mayonnaise, jalapeños and juice, chives, salt, and pepper. Spoon the yolk mixture into a pastry bag and pipe it into each egg-white half, or spoon it into the halves.

For the frisée salad: Tear the frisée into bite-sized pieces (you should have about 8 cups). In a medium skillet, cook the bacon over medium-high heat until crisp and browned, 8 to 10 minutes. Remove from the heat. Using a slotted spoon, transfer the bacon to paper towels and discard all but 2 tablespoons of fat from the pan. Add the shallot, mustard, and vinegar to the pan and whisk to blend. Gradually whisk in the oil until emulsified. Season with salt and pepper. Add the warm dressing and bacon to the frisée and toss .

To serve, divide the salad among 4 salad plates. Top each salad with 3 deviled egg halves, garnish with chives, and serve.
*Makes 4 first-course servings*

**Wine Pairing:** Dry Creek Valley or Alexander Valley Sauvignon Blanc

6 slices apple wood–smoked bacon,
    cut into ¼-inch-wide sticks (lardons)
1 tablespoon olive oil
8 ounces Yukon Gold potatoes, peeled and
    cut into ½-inch dice
½ cup thinly sliced shallots

**Vinaigrette**
⅓ cup reserved hot bacon fat (above) plus
    olive oil, if needed
1½ tablespoons sherry vinegar
2 teaspoons brown sugar
1 clove garlic, minced
1 teaspoon Dijon mustard
Freshly ground pepper to taste

½ teaspoon cream of tartar
4 large eggs
8 cups frisée or curly endive, small yellow
    and pale green leaves only, rinsed and
    spun dry
¼ cup chopped fresh flat-leaf parsley

In a medium skillet, sauté the lardons over medium heat until crisp and brown, 8 to 10 minutes. Drain the fat from the pan into a glass measuring cup and reserve. Using a slotted spoon, transfer the lardons to paper towels to drain. Add the olive oil, potatoes, and shallots to the hot pan and sauté until tender, 6 to 8 minutes. Remove from the heat and set aside.

For the vinaigrette: Add olive oil to the reserved bacon fat if necessary to make ⅓ cup. In a small bowl, combine the bacon fat, sherry vinegar, brown sugar, garlic, mustard, and 3 grinds of pepper. Whisk until well combined. Set aside and keep warm.

In a deep sauté pan over medium heat, bring 2 inches of water to a simmer. Add the cream of tartar and stir to dissolve. Break each egg into a small bowl and gently slide the eggs, one at a time, into the simmering water. Poach until the whites are firm but the yolks are still runny, 5 to 7 minutes. Using a slotted spatula, transfer the eggs to a plate.

In a large bowl, toss the frisée with the vinaigrette. Add the lardons, potatoes and shallots, and parsley. Toss again and divide among 4 serving plates. Top each with a poached egg and serve. *Makes 4 first-course servings*

**Wine Pairing:** Dry Creek Valley or Russian River Valley Sauvignon Blanc

33

## DUNGENESS CRAB–STUFFED AVOCADO WITH MANGO AND RED CHILE DRESSING

*This is a spin on the lunch entrée of an avocado filled with bay shrimp salad. Living on the West Coast, we are lucky enough to enjoy fresh Dungeness crab during the winter and early spring, while avocados grow year-round here. The mango and red chile dressing give this spark.*

### DUNGENESS CRAB

34  *The sea-sweet Dungeness crab is native to West Coast waters and is typically available from late November through June. December-caught Dungies are the largest and feistiest—signs that their shells, legs, and claws contain lots of meaty, succulent flesh. By mid-January, the crabs get smaller and may be missing claws. Crab can be prepared with various seasonings, yet a boiled crab picked apart and eaten with the hands is sublime; crab cakes are a more elegant, yet just as delicious, way to enjoy Dungeness crab.*

*I've become known for my crab cakes, so much so that our local food writer, who rates restaurants on a four-star scale, said that for this dish, he just holds the asterisk key down forever on his keyboard. The key to the crab cakes is to use the freshest Dungeness crab possible, and Best Foods mayonnaise (called Hellman's on the East Coast).*

**Red Chile Dressing**
½ cup mayonnaise
¼ cup Mae Ploy Sweet Chilli Sauce
Grated zest and juice of 2 limes
¼ teaspoon Tabasco sauce
1 tablespoon minced fresh chives
Kosher salt and freshly ground pepper
    to taste

**Crab Salad**
2 ripe avocados, halved lengthwise and
    pitted
1 ripe mango, peeled and cut from the pit
8 ounces fresh lump Dungeness crabmeat,
    picked over for shell
2 tablespoons minced fresh chives
Kosher salt and freshly ground pepper
    to taste

For the red chile dressing: In a small bowl, combine the mayonnaise, chilli sauce, lime zest and juice, Tabasco sauce, and chives. Stir to blend. Season with salt and pepper.

For the crab salad: Scoop the flesh from each avocado half, reserving the skin. Cut the avocado flesh and the mango flesh into ¼-inch dice. In a medium bowl, combine the crab, mango, and chives. Add all but about ¼ cup dressing and mix gently to coat. Gently fold in the diced avocado. Place 1 avocado skin on each of 4 plates, spoon crab salad into each half (you may have extra salad), and drizzle with the remaining dressing. *Makes 4 first-course servings*

**Wine Pairing:** Sonoma County Viognier

36

**Sherry Mayonnaise**
¾ cup mayonnaise, preferably Best Foods or
    Hellman's brand
2 teaspoons sherry vinegar
½ teaspoon sweet Hungarian paprika
Pinch of cayenne pepper

**Crab Cakes**
12 ounces fresh lump crabmeat, picked over
    for shells
½ cup mayonnaise, preferably Best Foods
    (or Hellman's)
3 tablespoons finely chopped red bell pepper
3 tablespoons finely chopped celery
2 tablespoons finely chopped red onion
1 tablespoon chopped fresh flat-leaf parsley
1 tablespoon fresh lemon juice
Kosher salt and freshly ground pepper
    to taste
About 1½ cups panko (Japanese bread
    crumbs)
About 1½ cups rice bran oil or canola oil
    for frying

For the mayonnaise: In a small bowl,
combine all the ingredients and stir to blend.
Cover and refrigerate for up to 2 weeks.

For the crab cakes: In a medium bowl,
combine the crabmeat, mayonnaise, bell
pepper, celery, onion, parsley, lemon juice,
salt, and pepper; mix well. Add the panko
gradually, a few tablespoons at a time, until
the consistency is dry and slightly tacky to the
touch. Form into 8 cakes about 2½ inches
wide and coat with more panko.

In a large skillet, heat ¼ inch oil over high
heat until it shimmers. Add the crab cakes,
working in batches if necessary to avoid
crowding pan. Cook until nicely browned,
about 3 minutes on each side. Using a slotted
metal spatula, transfer to paper towels to
drain briefly. Place 2 crab cakes on each of
4 salad plates, and serve with the sherry
mayonnaise on the side. *Makes 4 first-course
servings*

**Wine Pairing:** Carneros or Russian River
Valley Chardonnay

37

## ZINFANDEL-GLAZED BEEF SHORT RIBS WITH HORSERADISH MASHED POTATOES AND BACON-BRAISED BRUSSELS SPROUTS

*This is a real "meat and potatoes" winter dinner. Marinating the short ribs overnight makes a big difference in this dish, and adding horseradish to the mashed potatoes helps cut some of the fattiness of the ribs. As a kid, I was different from my friends in that I loved Brussels sprouts. My grandfather had a farm that grew them.*

My wife, Regina, loves this winter dinner. It takes a long time to prepare, but is well worth it. The slow braising of the ribs turns the meat tender and juicy, sending an aromatic waft through the house. When the weather turns chilly, we get reminders from friends that it's time to return the ribs to the menu.

## BRAISED SHORT RIBS WITH HORSERADISH CRÈME FRAÎCHE, MASHED POTATOES, AND SAUTÉED SPINACH,

## ZINFANDEL-GLAZED BEEF SHORT RIBS WITH HORSERADISH MASHED POTATOES

## AND BACON-BRAISED BRUSSELS SPROUTS

### Short Ribs

Four 3-bone racks beef short ribs,
    cut 2 inches thick (about 4 pounds)
Salt and freshly ground pepper to taste
About 3 tablespoons Zin Dry Rub (page 128)
3 tablespoons canola oil
2 poblano chiles, seeded, deribbed, and
    chopped
2 yellow onions, chopped
2 stalks celery, chopped
4 cloves garlic, sliced
3 cups Zinfandel or other dry red wine
4 cups chicken stock or broth
2 cups homemade or purchased
    barbecue sauce

### Brussels Sprouts

4 slices bacon, diced
1 yellow onion, chopped
1 cup chicken stock or broth
¼ cup dry sherry
1 teaspoon minced fresh thyme
1 pound Brussels sprouts, halved
2 tablespoons chopped fresh flat-leaf parsley
Kosher salt and freshly ground pepper
    to taste

### Horseradish Mashed Potatoes

4 Idaho potatoes (about 3 pounds), peeled
    and cut into quarters
1 cup heavy cream
4 tablespoons unsalted butter
2 tablespoons grated fresh horseradish root
    or prepared horseradish
Kosher salt to taste

For the short ribs: season the meat generously with salt, pepper, and dry rub. Cover and refrigerate for 8 hours or overnight.

Preheat the oven to 350°F. In a large Dutch oven, heat the oil over high heat. Add the ribs and cook, turning as needed, until well browned all over, 8 to 10 minutes total. Using tongs, transfer the ribs to paper towels and drain all but 1 tablespoon of the fat from the pan. Reduce the heat to medium and add the chiles, onions, celery, and garlic. Sauté until lightly browned, 8 to 10 minutes. Add the wine and stir to scrape up the browned bits from the bottom of the pan. Add the stock and barbecue sauce and bring to a boil. Return the ribs to the pan, cover, and braise in the oven until meat is very tender, 2 to 2½ hours.

Transfer the ribs to a platter and tent loosely with aluminum foil. Skim the fat from the pan sauce and pour the sauce through a fine-mesh sieve into a bowl; discard the vegetables. Return the sauce and meat to the pan and warm over medium-low heat until heated through. Remove from the heat and keep warm.

For the Brussels sprouts: In a large skillet, cook the bacon over medium heat until crisp and browned, 6 to 8 minutes. Drain all but 2 tablespoons of fat from the pan. Add the onion and Brussels sprouts and cook, stirring, until the onion is translucent, 5 to 6 minutes. Add the stock, sherry, and thyme. Bring to a boil, reduce the heat to low, and simmer until the Brussels sprouts are tender, about 10 minutes. Stir in the parsley and season with salt and pepper to taste. Remove from the heat and keep warm.

Meanwhile, for the mashed potatoes: Put the potatoes in a large pot and add cold water to cover. Bring to a boil over high heat. Reduce the heat to a simmer and cook until very tender when pierced, about 20 minutes. While the potatoes are cooking, in a small saucepan, combine the cream, butter, and horseradish. Cook over low heat until the butter is melted, 5 minutes. Drain the potatoes and return to the warm pan. Mash with a potato masher, gradually adding the hot horseradish cream. Season with salt.

To serve, spoon mounds of Brussels sprouts and potatoes onto 4 dinner plates. Top each with a short rib and spoon the pan sauce alongside. *Makes 4 main-course servings*

**Wine Pairing:** Sonoma County Zinfandel

### Horseradish Crème Fraîche

½ cup crème fraîche
1 teaspoon prepared horseradish, or to taste
Salt to taste

### Braised Short Ribs

6 short rib pieces (5 to 6 inches long; about 4 pounds total)
3 tablespoons kosher salt, plus more to taste
⅛ ounce dried porcini mushrooms
3 tablespoons rice bran oil or canola oil
2 carrots, peeled and cut into 1-inch chunks
1 yellow onion, cut into 1-inch chunks
2 stalks celery, cut into 1-inch chunks
2 tablespoons tomato paste
½ cup ruby port
3 cups dry red wine
4 cups beef broth or veal stock
2 bay leaves
3 sprigs thyme
6 black peppercorns
1 pound mixed wild mushrooms, trimmed and cut into ½-inch pieces

### Mashed Potatoes

3 pounds Yukon Gold Potatoes, peeled and cut into 2-inch chunks
½ cup heavy cream
3 tablespoons unsalted butter
Salt and freshly ground pepper to taste

### Sautéed Spinach

3 tablespoons unsalted butter
3 shallots, thinly sliced
3 cloves garlic, thinly sliced
2 bunches spinach, stemmed and rinsed
Salt and freshly ground pepper to taste

For the horseradish crème fraîche: In a small bowl, combine all the ingredients and stir to blend. Cover and refrigerate for up to 8 hours.

For the short ribs: Rub the meat all over with the 3 tablespoons kosher salt; cover and refrigerate overnight.

In a blender, process the dried porcini mushrooms until they form a fine powder. Set aside

Preheat the oven to 300°F. Using a paper towel, wipe the salt from the short ribs. In a large roasting pan or Dutch oven, heat the oil over high heat until it shimmers. Add the short ribs to the pan, working in batches if necessary (do not crowd pan), and cook until well browned, about 4 minutes on each side. Using tongs, transfer to paper towels to drain. Discard all but 1 tablespoon fat from the pan. Return the pan to medium heat and add the carrots, onion, celery, and mushroom powder. Sauté for 5 minutes. Add the tomato paste and cook for 1 minute. Add the port and red wine and cook, stirring occasionally, for 8 minutes. Add the broth, short ribs, bay leaves, thyme, and peppercorns and bring to a boil. Cover the pan tightly with aluminum foil or a lid and bake until meat is very tender, 3 to 3½ hours. Remove from the oven.

Transfer the meat to a plate and cover loosely with aluminum foil. Strain the cooking liquid (discard the solids), and skim and discard the fat. Return to the pan and add the mushrooms. Set over medium-high heat and cook, stirring occasionally, until dark in color, about 30 minutes. Reduce the heat and add the short ribs to pan; cook until heated through. Season with salt to taste. Remove from the heat and keep warm.

For the mashed potatoes: Put the potatoes in a large pot and add cold water to cover. Bring to a boil, reduce the heat to a lively simmer, and cook until potatoes are tender, 20 to 30 minutes. Meanwhile, in a small saucepan, heat the cream and butter over low heat until the butter is melted. Drain the potatoes well and return to the pan. Mash the potatoes with a potato masher and slowly drizzle in the hot cream mixture. Season with salt and pepper. Remove from the heat and keep warm.

For the sautéed spinach: In a large skillet, melt the butter over medium-high heat and cook until lightly browned, 1 to 2 minutes. Add the shallots and garlic and cook, stirring, until golden, about 2 minutes. Add the spinach until the pan is full and cover until the spinach is wilted, 2 to 3 minutes; repeat, adding the remaining spinach in batches. Season with salt and pepper. Transfer to a colander and press with the back of a spoon to drain off the excess liquid. Set aside and keep warm.

To serve, spoon a mound of mashed potatoes and sautéed spinach onto each dinner plate. Add a short rib, surround with the liquid, and dollop with the horseradish crème fraîche.
*Makes 6 main-course servings*

**Wine Pairing:** Sonoma County Syrah

41

## LEMON-HERB ROASTED CHICKEN
## WITH ONION AND SAGE CREAM GRAVY,
## BRAISED CABBAGE, AND BISCUITS

*Forget about buying boneless, skinless chicken breasts or other packaged parts. Buy the whole chicken and take the time to properly roast it. For this recipe, you can cook the cabbage and prep the biscuits while the chicken is cooking. Bake the biscuits when the chicken comes out of the oven.*

**FULTON VALLEY FARMS**

42 *This poultry supplier is based in Fulton, a wide spot in the road between Santa Rosa and Windsor in Sonoma County. Restaurant chefs and home cooks prize its birds for their juicy flavor and organic diet. The chickens are raised by Fulton Valley member ranchers in California's Central Valley and delivered to Sonoma County for processing and delivery.*

This dish is a fun takeoff on pasta alla carbonara, using spaghetti squash instead of pasta.
Once baked, the squash separates into yellow-gold strands that look just like spaghetti.
We always brine our chicken, as it keeps the meat moist and adds flavor.
Salt and sugar are mandatory brine seasonings, although you can easily vary the others.

**PAN-ROASTED CHICKEN BREAST
WITH SPAGHETTI SQUASH "CARBONARA"**

### Roast Chicken

1 lemon
1 whole chicken (3 to 3½ pounds), giblets
    removed, rinsed inside and out
Kosher salt and freshly ground pepper
    to taste
1 clove garlic
2 sprigs each rosemary, sage, and thyme
¼ cup extra-virgin olive oil

### Braised Cabbage

2 tablespoons olive oil
½ cup diced ham
1 yellow onion, chopped
1 small head green cabbage (about
    2 pounds), cored and thinly sliced
1 cup water
Salt and freshly ground pepper to taste

### Biscuits

2 cups all-purpose flour
1 tablespoon baking powder
1 teaspoon kosher salt
6 tablespoons cold unsalted butter
⅔ cup heavy cream
⅓ cup milk, plus more for brushing

### Onion and Sage Cream Gravy

1 yellow onion, thinly sliced
1 tablespoon chopped fresh sage
1 cup heavy cream
1 cup chicken stock or broth
Salt and freshly ground pepper to taste

For the roast chicken: Preheat the oven to 450°F. Grate the zest from the lemon and reserve. Season the body cavity of the chicken with salt and pepper and place the garlic, lemon, and 1 sprig of each herb in the cavity. Tie the legs together with kitchen twine. Chop the leaves from the remaining herb sprigs and, in a small bowl, mix with the reserved lemon zest and the olive oil. Rub the olive oil mixture all over the chicken and sprinkle with salt and pepper to taste.

Place the chicken, breast side up, on a V-shaped rack in a roasting pan and roast for 15 minutes. Reduce the heat to 350°F and continue to roast until the juices run clear when a thigh is pierced and a thermometer inserted into the thickest part of the breast registers 170°F, 35 to 45 minutes longer. Increase the oven temperature to 450°F. Transfer the chicken to a carving board and tent loosely with aluminum foil. Reserve the pan to make the gravy.

For the braised cabbage: While the chicken is roasting, heat the oil in a Dutch oven or heavy casserole over medium-high heat. Add the ham and onion and sauté until the onion is browned, 8 to 10 minutes. Add the cabbage and water, reduce the heat to a simmer, cover, and cook until cabbage is tender, 45 minutes. Season with salt and pepper. Remove from the heat and set aside.

For the biscuits: In a medium bowl, combine the flour, salt, and baking powder. Stir with a whisk to blend. Using a pastry blender or

two dinner knives, cut the butter into the flour until the mixture resembles coarse meal. Add the cream and the ⅓ cup milk and stir until the mixture comes together. On a floured board, knead the dough a few times, then form it into a ball. Using a floured rolling pin, roll the dough out to a ½-inch thickness. Cut out rounds with a 2-inch round cutter, pressing the cutter straight down without twisting it. Reroll the scraps and cut out more biscuits. Place on an ungreased baking sheet, brush the tops of the biscuits with milk, and bake until golden brown and well risen, 14 to 16 minutes.

For the gravy: Pour off all but 3 tablespoons of the fat from the reserved roasting pan. Place the pan on the stove top over medium heat and add the onion and sage. Sauté until browned, 8 to 10 minutes. Add the cream and stock and bring to a boil. Stir to scrape up the browned bits from the bottom of the pan. Reduce the heat to a simmer and cook, stirring often, until the gravy is thick, 6 to 7 minutes. Season with salt and pepper. Remove from the heat and keep warm.

To serve, reheat the cabbage over low heat. Carve the chicken and divide among 4 plates. Pour gravy over each portion, place a serving of cabbage next to the chicken, and serve with the biscuits. *Makes 4 main-course servings*

**Wine Pairings:** Sonoma County Chenin Blanc or Sauvignon Blanc

**Brined Chicken Breasts**
2 cloves garlic
4 sprigs thyme
6 black peppercorns
¼ cup kosher salt
1 tablespoon sugar
4 cups water
4 boneless, skin-on chicken breasts,
  about 8 ounces each (see Note)
1 tablespoon canola oil

1 spaghetti squash (about 2½ pounds)

**Carbonara Sauce**
3 slices apple wood–smoked bacon,
  cut into ½-inch pieces
1½ cups heavy cream
3 cloves garlic, minced
2 cups baby spinach leaves
½ cup grated Parmesan cheese
1 large egg yolk, beaten
Kosher salt and freshly ground pepper
  to taste
3 tablespoons chopped fresh flat-leaf parsley

For the brined chicken breasts: In a saucepan, combine the garlic, thyme, peppercorns, salt, sugar, and water. Bring to a boil over high heat, stirring until the salt and sugar are dissolved. Remove from the heat and let cool, then add several ice cubes until thoroughly chilled. Put the chicken in a bowl and pour the brine over it. Cover and refrigerate for at least 12 or up to 24 hours.

Preheat the oven to 425°F. Cut the squash in half lengthwise and scoop out the seeds. Lightly oil a rimmed baking sheet and place the squash halves on it, cut side down. Roast until tender, about 45 minutes. Remove from the oven and let stand until cool enough to handle. With a spoon, scoop out the squash flesh; it will come out in long strands, similar to spaghetti. Set aside, or cover and refrigerate for up to 1 day before using.

Increase the oven temperature to 450°F. Drain the chicken breasts, pat dry, and let come to room temperature. In a large ovenproof skillet, heat the oil over medium-high heat. Add the breasts, skin side down, and cook until browned, 6 to 8 minutes. Turn the chicken over, transfer the pan to the oven and roast until opaque throughout, about 16 to 18 minutes.

Meanwhile, for the spaghetti squash carbonara: In a large skillet, sauté the bacon over medium heat until the fat is rendered and the bacon is browned, 5 to 6 minutes. Using a slotted spoon, transfer the bacon to paper towels to drain. Add the cream and garlic to the pan with the bacon fat and cook, stirring, until cream is reduced by half, about 6 minutes. Add the spaghetti squash and stir until coated and heated through. Add the spinach to the pan and stir until wilted, 1 minute. Reduce the heat to low and stir in the Parmesan, egg yolk, reserved bacon, salt, and pepper and cook for 1 minute, stirring constantly. Stir in the parsley.

To serve, divide the spaghetti squash carbonara among 4 dinner plates. Top each with a roasted chicken breast and serve at once. *Makes 4 main-course servings*

**Wine Pairing:** Sonoma County Chardonnay

Note: At Syrah, we use skin-on chicken breasts that have been deboned with the exception of the first wing joint, which is left on—a common cut in restaurants that's referred to as the "airline" cut. Unfortunately, this cut is not generally available to home cooks, unless you buy whole chickens and cut them up yourself, or convince a friendly butcher to do it for you.

45

## MEYER LEMON CHEESECAKE WITH COCONUT CRUST AND BLOOD ORANGE SYRUP

*Meyer lemons and blood oranges add spark to winter menus and are both in season during the winter months. Coconut gives this cheesecake an all-American flavor. Serve it with a bowl of blood orange syrup on the side and let guests drizzle it on their slices of cheesecake to their taste.*

### MEYER LEMONS

*A cross between the common Eureka lemon and a mandarin orange, Meyer lemons are sweeter and less acidic than other varieties, and more aromatic, with a thinner, smoother skin and pith. In color, they're yellow with a subtle orange tinge, and they tend to yield more juice than other lemons. Meyer lemons, grown in China for centuries, were brought to the United States in 1908 by botanist Frank Meyer, who lent them his name. The season runs from early November to June, and during that time, the semipuckery fruit is easy to find in wine country stores, at farmers' markets, and in residents' backyards. Meyer lemons work beautifully in dishes where a lemony flavor with lower acidity is desired, such as in desserts. They also add a mellow tang to vinaigrettes and olive oils.*

*This recipe is an Italian twist on the classic New York cheesecake: I use Italian Amarena cherries in syrup as a garnish and some mascarpone along with the cream cheese because it's a bit lighter and gives the dish a more elegant texture. We get our mascarpone from the local Clover Stornetta Dairy, a company committed to sustainable agriculture and pristine products.*

**CLOVER STORNETTA DAIRY**

*Anyone driving Highway 101 in Northern California in the last forty years has likely seen Clover Stornetta's billboards featuring its cartoon cow, Clo. Who could forget her slightly smiling portrait as "Moona Lisa" or her portrayal of a judge holding a "Supreme Quart" of Clover milk? Clover Stornetta has delivered quality dairy products, many of them organic, to restaurants and grocers since Gene Benedetti founded the company in Petaluma in 1977. Clover Stornetta sells dairy goods to hundreds of retail stores and restaurants in Northern California; dine in wine country and there is a good chance the cream and butter you're served are from that firm.*

47

**Meyer Lemon Curd**

2 teaspoons grated Meyer lemon zest
⅓ cup fresh Meyer lemon juice
¼ cup sugar
1 large egg, beaten
4 tablespoons unsalted butter,
  cut into chunks

1 cup sweetened shredded dried coconut
Approximately 45 vanilla wafers
  (one-half of a 12-ounce box)
4 tablespoons unsalted butter, melted
Pinch of salt

**Filling**

24 ounces cream cheese at room
  temperature
¾ cup sugar
1 tablespoon grated Meyer lemon zest
½ cup fresh Meyer lemon juice
½ teaspoon kosher salt
4 large eggs

**Blood Orange Syrup**

2 cups fresh blood orange juice
½ cup sugar

For the lemon curd: In a heatproof bowl set over a pan of barely simmering water (but not touching the water), whisk the lemon zest and juice, sugar, and egg together. Gradually stir in the butter and cook, stirring, until thick enough to coat the back of a spoon, 6 to 8 minutes. Strain through a fine-mesh sieve into a bowl and let cool. Cover and refrigerate for at least 1 hour or up to 2 days.

Preheat the oven to 350°F. Spread the coconut on a rimmed baking sheet and toast, stirring occasionally, until golden, 6 to 8 minutes. Wrap the outside bottom and sides of a 9-inch springform pan well in a double layer of aluminum foil. In a food processor, process the vanilla wafers until fine crumbs form. Add ½ cup of the toasted coconut and the butter and salt, and pulse to combine. Press the crumb mixture into the bottom of the springform pan. Place in oven and bake until the crust looks dry, 12 to 15 minutes. Transfer to a wire rack and let cool.

For the filling: Preheat the oven to 350°F. Using a stand mixer fitted with the paddle attachment, beat the cream cheese and sugar together until smooth. Add the lemon zest, lemon juice, and salt and beat well. Beat in the eggs on low speed, one at a time, just until combined. Pour the batter into the springform pan. Gently top with dollops of the lemon curd and use a toothpick to create a swirl pattern.

Place the springform pan in a shallow baking pan. Add hot water to come halfway up the side of the springform pan. Transfer the water bath and springform pan to the oven and bake 45 to 50 minutes, or until all but a 2-inch area in the center is completely set. Immediately run a sharp knife around rim of pan to prevent cracking as cheesecake cools. Remove from the water bath and transfer to a wire rack to cool at room temperature, 1 hour. Cover and refrigerate for at least 4 hours or up to 24 hours.

For the blood orange syrup: In a small saucepan, combine the orange juice and sugar. Cook over high heat, stirring until the sugar is dissolved, then cook until reduced by half, 15 to 20 minutes. Remove from the heat and let cool. Cover and refrigerate for at least 1 hour or up to 3 days.

To serve, run a thin-bladed knife around the edges of the springform pan and remove the pan rim. With a cupped hand, press the remaining toasted coconut into the sides of the cheesecake. Cut the cheesecake into 12 wedges. Place each on a dessert plate and drizzle with the blood orange syrup.
*Makes 12 servings*

**Wine Pairing:** Sonoma County late-harvest Riesling

### Crust

1 box (12 ounces) vanilla wafers
6 tablespoons unsalted butter, melted

### Mascarpone Filling

20 ounces cream cheese at room
  temperature
8 ounces mascarpone cheese at room
  temperature
1 cup sugar
3 large eggs
1 teaspoon vanilla extract
1 teaspoon fresh lemon juice
Pinch of salt

### Topping

1 cup sour cream
¼ cup sugar
1 teaspoon vanilla extract
1 teaspoon fresh lemon juice
Pinch of salt

1 jar (8 ounces) of Amarena cherries
  in syrup
Fresh mint sprigs

For the crust: Preheat the oven to 350°F. In a food processor, grind the wafers to fine crumbs. With the machine running, gradually add the butter and pulse until well coated. Reserve ¾ cup of the wafer mixture; press the remainder into the bottom and slightly up the sides of a 9-inch springform pan. Set the pan on a baking sheet and bake for 10 minutes. Remove from the oven, leaving the oven on, and let the crust cool on a wire rack for 15 minutes.

For the filling: Using an electric mixer on medium speed, beat the cream cheese, mascarpone, and sugar together until very creamy, 2 minutes. Add the eggs, one at a time, and beat on low speed until incorporated; beat in the vanilla, lemon juice, and salt. Pour into the cooled crust and bake until the center jiggles just slightly when shaken, 30 to 35 minutes. Remove from the oven, leaving the oven on, and let cool on a wire rack for 20 minutes.

For the topping: In a small bowl, combine all the ingredients and stir until smooth. Pour over the cooled cheesecake and bake for 10 minutes. Remove from the oven and let cool slightly on a wire rack. Sprinkle the top of the cake with the reserved cookie mixture, if desired. Let cool completely, then refrigerate for least 6 hours or up to 48 hours.

To serve, use a long, thin knife to cut the cheesecake into wedges, cleaning the blade with hot water after each cut. Garnish each plate with 3 to 4 Amarena cherries, a tablespoon of cherry syrup, and a mint sprig. *Makes 10 to 12 servings*

**Wine Pairing:** Sonoma County Muscat or sec (moderately sweet) sparkling wine

49

## CHOCOLATE AND PEANUT BUTTER MOUSSE LAYER CAKE

*As a kid, I didn't have much of a sweet tooth, but given the opportunity to pick a candy bar, my favorite was a Reese's peanut butter cup. Here's another winning combination of those two great tastes, chocolate and peanut butter.*

50

Who doesn't like peanut butter and chocolate? To push this dish over the top, serve it with chocolate ice cream. There are some things you just don't do halfway! Dessert should be all about decadence; if you're not in the mood, just have a cup of coffee or a glass of dessert wine and call it a night.

# CHOCOLATE AND PEANUT BUTTER MOUSSE LAYER CAKE

## Chocolate Cake Layers

2 ounces bittersweet chocolate, chopped
1 cup hot coffee
2 cups granulated sugar
1¾ cups all-purpose flour
1 cup unsweetened cocoa powder
1¼ teaspoons baking soda
½ teaspoon baking powder
¾ teaspoon salt
2 large eggs
½ cup canola oil
1 cup buttermilk
½ teaspoon vanilla extract

## Peanut Butter Mousse

6 ounces cream cheese at room temperature
2 cups confectioners' sugar, sifted
1⅓ cups creamy peanut butter
1⅓ cups heavy cream

## Chocolate Frosting

1 cup heavy cream
2 tablespoons granulated sugar
2 tablespoons light corn syrup
1 pound bittersweet chocolate, chopped
4 tablespoons unsalted butter

For the chocolate cake layers: Preheat the oven to 300°F. Butter and flour two 9-inch round cake pans; knock out the excess flour. Line the bottom of each pan with a round of parchment paper.

In a small bowl, combine the chocolate and coffee. Let stand for 5 minutes, then stir until chocolate is melted and the mixture is smooth.

Sift the sugar, flour, cocoa powder, baking soda, baking powder, and salt together into a medium bowl.

Using an electric mixer on medium speed, beat the eggs until pale and slightly thickened. Gradually beat in the oil, buttermilk, vanilla, and chocolate mixture; beat until well combined. Gradually beat in the flour mixture until just combined, scraping down the sides of the bowl as needed.

Divide the batter between the prepared pans and bake until a toothpick inserted in the center comes out clean, about 50 minutes. Let cool in the pans for 5 minutes, then unmold onto wire racks and peel off the paper. Turn the cake layers right side up on the racks and let cool completely.

For the peanut butter mousse: Using a stand mixer fitted with the paddle attachment, beat the cream cheese and confectioners' sugar together until soft and creamy. Beat in the peanut butter just until incorporated. In a deep bowl, whip the cream until soft peaks form; fold into the peanut butter mixture until blended. Cover and refrigerate for at least 30 minutes or up to 4 hours.

For the chocolate frosting: In a medium saucepan, combine the cream, sugar, and corn syrup. Bring to a boil over medium heat, whisking until the sugar is dissolved. Remove from the heat and add the chocolate; whisk until the chocolate is melted, then whisk in the butter. Let cool.

To assemble the cake, use a long, serrated knife to cut each cake layer in half horizontally. Place 1 cake layer half on a cake plate and spread with one-third of the peanut butter mousse. Top with a second layer and repeat until all the cake layers are stacked. Spread the frosting evenly over top and sides of cake; if it is too thin to coat the sides evenly, refrigerate the frosting briefly to thicken. Using a serrated knife, cut the cake into wedges and serve. *Makes 10 to 12 servings*

**Wine Pairing:** Tawny port–style dessert wine or late-harvest Zinfandel

52

### Chocolate Ice Cream

2 cups half-and-half

⅓ cup plus 2 tablespoons unsweetened cocoa powder

½ vanilla bean, split lengthwise, or 1½ teaspoons vanilla extract

2 ounces semisweet chocolate, chopped

4 large egg yolks

½ cup sugar

### Chocolate Crumb Crust

8 ounces chocolate sandwich cookies, such as Oreos

3 tablespoons unsalted butter, melted

### Peanut Butter Filling

1 cup heavy cream

8 ounces cream cheese at room temperature

1 cup creamy peanut butter

½ cup sugar

1 teaspoon vanilla extract

### Chocolate Glaze

⅓ cup heavy cream

2 tablespoons unsalted butter

4 ounces bittersweet chocolate, finely chopped

For the ice cream: In a small saucepan, whisk the half-and-half and cocoa powder together until smooth. If using the vanilla bean, scrape the seeds into the half-and-half mixture and add the pods. Cook over medium-high heat until bubbles form around the edges of the pan. Remove from the heat and remove the vanilla pods; reserve the pods for other uses. Add the chopped chocolate and stir until smooth. Stir in the vanilla extract, if using.

In a heatproof bowl, whisk the egg yolks and sugar until fluffy and pale in color. Gradually whisk the hot half-and-half mixture into the egg yolk mixture.

Place the bowl over a saucepan of barely simmering water (but not touching the water) and, stirring constantly, cook until the custard is thick enough to coat the back of a spoon or registers 170°F, 12 to 14 minutes. Immediately remove the custard from the heat and continue to stir for a few minutes; add the vanilla extract, if using.

Cover and let cool to room temperature, strain through a fine-mesh sieve, then chill until very cold, at least 8 hours. Pour into an ice-cream maker and freeze according to manufacturer's instructions. The ice cream may be served soft when freshly churned; for firmer ice cream, cover tightly and freeze for up to 3 days.

For the crust: Preheat the oven to 350°F. In a food processor, grind the cookies to fine crumbs. Add the butter and pulse to coat. Press the mixture all the way up the sides of an 8-inch pie dish into an even ¼-inch layer. Bake until dry in appearance, 10 minutes. Remove from the oven and let cool on a wire rack.

For the filling: In a deep bowl, beat the whipped cream until stiff peaks form. In the bowl of a stand mixer fitted with the paddle attachment, beat the cream cheese, peanut butter, sugar, and vanilla on medium speed until smooth. Stir in half the whipped cream, then carefully fold in the remaining whipped cream until no white streaks remain. Smooth the mixture into the cooled crust, cover with plastic wrap, and refrigerate until firm, 4 hours.

For the glaze: In a small saucepan, bring the cream and butter to a simmer over low heat. Remove from the heat, add the chocolate, and stir until smooth. Let cool to lukewarm. Pour evenly over the chilled pie filling and refrigerate until set, 30 minutes.

To serve, cut the pie into wedges and top with a scoop of the ice cream. *Makes 8 to 10 servings*

**Wine Pairing:** Tawny port–style dessert wine

53

*Grapevines turn from withered stick figures into green flowering machines;*
*fruit trees blossom, strawberries and lettuces are ripe for the picking, and wine*
*country is abuzz with birds, beneficial insects, and wine tasters.*

*T*he land awakens from its winter hibernation and bursts into springtime energy. Daytime temperatures are warm, though nights remain chilly, so frost is still a threat to flowering plants, including grapevines. Spring showers keep the fields refreshed yet do relatively little, if any, damage. Apple, pear, and cherry trees ignite with colorful blossoms; sage, thyme, oregano, rosemary, and lavender show their savory selves; and strawberries, pea shoots, dozens of lettuce types, spring onions, fava beans, and green garlic reenter the minds of creative chefs. Sturdy artichokes and tender asparagus arrive, and spring lamb is the meat of choice for most chefs, with duck a close second.

## SPRING GREENS SALAD WITH BELLWETHER FARMS PEPATO CHEESE, CANDIED PECANS, AND PICKLED ONION

*Our spring greens salad has been on the menu at Zin since the day we opened. The only difference here is that we've added Bellwether Farms pepato cheese. This Sonoma County sheep's milk cheese is one of my absolute favorites. The whole peppercorns in the cheese are a nice contrast to the candied pecans.*

### BELLWETHER FARMS

*There is nothing like a bold, black-peppercorn-laced Bellwether Farms pepato cheese to perk up a spring greens salad. This aged sheep's milk cheese is made by Liam Callahan, who runs Bellwether Farms in western Sonoma County, along with his mother, Cindy. Cindy and her late husband, Ed, founded the farm in 1986, and it became the first sheep dairy in California. The Bellwether herd is a northern European breed called East Friesian, said to be one of the best milk-producing sheep in the world. Modeled somewhat after Italian pecorino pepato, Bellwether's pepato is less salty and less dry, yet provides an assertive peppery kick and a tangy finish. The Callahans also produce cow's milk and fresh cheeses, which find their way nationwide to restaurant menus and gourmet markets.*

*I've used a cucumber "bowl" for this salad since we opened the restaurant in 1999. It's an easy and elegant presentation and always wows our guests. Verjus is the unfermented juice of unripe wine grapes and a wine-friendly substitute for vinegar. My preferred goat cheese producer: Laura Chenel.*

**LAURA CHENEL'S CHÈVRE**

*Laura Chenel not only started the American goat cheese revolution, she retreated from it on her own terms. Chenel began making fresh goat's milk cheese, called chèvre in France, in Sonoma in 1979. Alice Waters of Chez Panisse restaurant in Berkeley discovered Chenel's cheese, put it on her menu, and soon Laura was not only a rock star in the world of fromage, she was among the first Sonoma County artisans to put the region on the world culinary map. In 2006, Chenel sold her company to Rians, a French cheese specialist. She continues to sell milk from her five hundred goats to Rians, which has kept her name on the cheeses.*

## SPRING GREENS SALAD WITH BELLWETHER FARMS PEPATO CHEESE, CANDIED PECANS, AND PICKLED ONION

**Pickled Red Onion**
1 cup rice wine vinegar
1 cup red wine vinegar
½ cup sugar
1 bay leaf
10 black peppercorns
Pinch of kosher salt
1 red onion, thinly sliced

**Candied Pecans**
2 cups maple syrup
1 cup pecan pieces
Kosher salt for sprinkling

**Mustard Vinaigrette**
1 tablespoon brown mustard,
   such as Gulden's
1 tablespoon minced shallot
1 tablespoon sherry vinegar
2 teaspoons minced fresh marjoram
2 teaspoons minced fresh flat-leaf parsley
1 clove garlic, minced
2 tablespoons extra-virgin olive oil
2 tablespoons canola oil
3 drops hot sauce, such as Tabasco
Kosher salt and freshly ground pepper
   to taste

8 cups mixed baby greens
Kosher salt and freshly ground pepper
   to taste
8 ounces Bellwether Farms pepato cheese,
   cut into 8 thin wedges (if unavailable,
   a Tuscan-style aged sheep's milk cheese
   may be substituted)

For the pickled red onion: In a small nonreactive saucepan, combine the vinegars, sugar, bay leaf, peppercorns, and salt. Bring to a boil over high heat. Put the onion slices in a nonreactive bowl and pour the vinegar mixture over them. Let cool. Cover and refrigerate for at least 4 hours or up to 1 week.

For the candied pecans: Preheat the oven to 300°F. In a small saucepan, combine the syrup and pecans. Bring to a simmer and cook for 30 minutes. Drain (reserving the syrup for another use) and spread the pecans on a baking sheet. Bake until dry and lightly browned, 30 minutes. Sprinkle lightly with salt.

For the vinaigrette: In a small bowl, whisk the mustard, shallot, vinegar, marjoram, parsley, and garlic together. Gradually whisk in the olive oil and canola oil. Season with the hot sauce, salt, and pepper.

In a large bowl, toss the greens with the vinaigrette to coat. Season with salt and pepper and toss again. Divide the greens among 4 salad plates and top each salad with some of the pickled onions and pecans. Place 2 cheese wedges alongside each salad and serve. *Makes 4 first-course servings*

**Wine Pairing:** Sonoma County Pinot Grigio or Sauvignon Blanc

1 cup balsamic vinegar

**Maple-Roasted Walnuts**
1 teaspoon unsalted butter
¼ cup pure maple syrup
1 cup walnuts

**Vinaigrette**
⅓ cup verjus
⅓ cup extra-virgin olive oil
1 tablespoon minced shallot
1 tablespoon chopped fresh mint
1 tablespoon chopped fresh flat-leaf parsley
1 tablespoon thinly sliced fresh chives
Kosher salt and freshly ground pepper
    to taste

¼ cup fresh or frozen green peas
4 spears asparagus, cut into ½-inch lengths,
    plus 8 thin asparagus spears, trimmed
1 English cucumber
4 cups mixed baby greens
¼ cup thinly sliced radishes
½ cup crumbled fresh goat cheese,
    such as Laura Chenel
2 ounces enoki mushrooms
4 edible flowers, such as pansies or
    nasturtiums
Extra-virgin olive oil for garnish

In a small saucepan, bring the vinegar to a boil over medium heat. Reduce the heat to a simmer and cook until reduced to ¼ cup, about 15 minutes. Let cool, cover, and refrigerate for up to 3 weeks.

For the walnuts: Preheat the oven to 325°F. In a small saucepan, melt the butter with the maple syrup over medium heat. Add the walnuts and stir to coat. Spread on a baking sheet and bake until lightly browned, 10 to 12 minutes. Line a second baking sheet with parchment paper and immediately pour the nuts onto the prepared pan. Let cool to room temperature. Cover airtight and store at room temperature until ready to use.

For the vinaigrette: In a small bowl, whisk the verjus, olive oil, shallot, and herbs together. Season with salt and pepper. Set aside.

Cook the peas in a medium saucepan of salted boiling water for 20 seconds. Using a slotted spoon or mesh strainer, transfer the peas to ice water to stop the cooking; drain and pat dry. Add the chopped asparagus and thin spears to the boiling water and cook until bright green, 30 seconds to 1 minute. Drain and plunge into ice water; drain again and pat dry.

Using a mandoline, thinly slice the cucumber into 8 lengthwise slices. Lay 2 strips flat on a work surface, overlapping by one-fourth of their length to form a very long strip, then bend them into a bowl shape. Set the bowl on a salad plate. Repeat to make a total of 4 bowls.

In a large bowl, combine the greens, peas, chopped asparagus, radishes, goat cheese, and maple walnuts. Add about half the vinaigrette and toss to coat; add more vinaigrette as desired, or reserve for other uses.

Divide the salad among the cucumber bowls. Using your fingers, make an indentation in the center of each salad and stand 2 asparagus spears, a few enoki mushrooms, and an edible flower in the center. Drizzle 5 dots of olive oil around the edges of the plate, put a drop of the reduced balsamic in the center of each dot, and serve. *Makes 4 first-course servings*

**Wine Pairing:** Dry Creek Valley or Russian River Valley Sauvignon Blanc

61

## GRILLED GULF SHRIMP COCKTAIL
## WITH CELERY SALAD
## AND ZIN COCKTAIL SAUCE

*It's always important to know where your food comes from. This is especially important when buying fish and seafood. When purchasing shrimp, avoid farm-raised shrimp and seek out wild-caught shrimp. I prefer Gulf shrimp, which not only taste better but are much better for the environment than their farm-raised cousins from Asia. The flavor of Gulf shrimp is not overpowered by the dry rub and spicy cocktail sauce in this great update of a classic shrimp cocktail.*

## PRAWN COCKTAIL WITH
## DAMN GOOD COCKTAIL SAUCE

*The trick to tender, great-tasting prawns is to steep them in a flavorful liquid, called a court bouillon. I learned this method from my dad and have used it for years. The cocktail sauce is, well, damn good.*

### Zin Cocktail Sauce

1 cup Zin Catsup (recipe follows)
1 tablespoon prepared horseradish
1 tablespoon minced fresh flat-leaf parsley

1 pound extra-large (16 to 20 count) fresh
    Gulf shrimp, shelled and deveined
1 tablespoon extra-virgin olive oil
1 tablespoon Zin Dry Rub (page 128)
Kosher salt and freshly ground pepper
    to taste

### Celery Salad

3 stalks celery, cut into thin diagonal slices
¼ cup thinly sliced red onion
2 tablespoons extra-virgin olive oil
1 teaspoon finely grated lemon zest
2 teaspoons fresh lemon juice
2 tablespoons chopped fresh flat-leaf
    parsley
Kosher salt and freshly ground pepper
    to taste

For the cocktail sauce: In a small bowl, stir all the ingredients together until blended. Set aside. The sauce can be made a day ahead, covered with plastic wrap, and kept in the refrigerator.

Prepare a hot fire in a charcoal grill, or preheat a gas grill to high. Soak 4 bamboo skewers in water for 30 minutes. Thread 4 shrimp onto each skewer. Brush with the olive oil and season with the dry rub, salt, and pepper. Grill, turning once, just until shrimp are evenly pink, about 4 minutes total; do not overcook.

For the celery salad: In a small bowl, combine the celery, onion, olive oil, lemon zest and juice, and parsley. Toss to coat and season with salt and pepper.

To serve, divide the celery salad among 4 salad plates. Top each with a grilled-shrimp skewer and serve with the cocktail sauce on the side. *Makes 4 first-course servings*

**Wine Pairing:** Sonoma County dry rosé

### Zin Catsup

Two 6-ounce cans tomato paste
½ cup dry red wine, preferably Zinfandel
¼ cup sugar
2 tablespoons apple cider vinegar
1½ tablespoons Sriracha hot sauce
2½ teaspoons onion powder
1 teaspoon garlic powder
1 teaspoon freshly ground black pepper
1 bay leaf
1 tablespoon kosher salt
¾ cup water

In a double boiler, combine all the ingredients and cook over simmering water, stirring often and adding water to the bottom of the double boiler as needed, until thickened, 1 hour. Strain through a fine-mesh sieve. Let cool. Store in the refrigerator for up to 1 week. *Makes 1½ cups*

64

**Cocktail Sauce**
½ cup catsup
1½ teaspoons prepared horseradish,
    or more to taste
1½ tablespoons fresh lemon juice
2 teaspoons chopped fresh flat-leaf parsley

**Court Bouillon**
1 cup dry white wine
6 black peppercorns
1 teaspoon fennel seeds
1 teaspoon dried tarragon
2 cloves garlic, crushed
1 tablespoon kosher salt
1 teaspoon sugar
6 cups water

1 pound extra-large shrimp (16 to 20 count)
    in the shell, rinsed
2 cups loosely packed mixed baby greens
Chives for garnish
1 lemon, cut into 4 wedges, for garnish

For the cocktail sauce: Combine all the ingredients and stir until smooth. Taste and add more horseradish if desired. Cover and refrigerate for at least 1 hour or up to 2 days.

For the court bouillon: In a large pot, combine all the ingredients. Bring to a boil over high heat and let cook for 5 minutes to blend the flavors.

Cut through the shells on the top of each shrimp and, with the tip of the knife, remove the dark vein. Put the shrimp in a large bowl and pour the hot court bouillon over them through a fine-mesh sieve (discard the solids). Let stand until the court bouillon is room temperature, about 30 to 45 minutes. Add ice cubes to chill the liquid and let stand in the ice bath for 15 minutes. Drain, peel the shells from the shrimp (leaving the tails on), and set aside.

To serve, fill 4 martini glasses with ½ cup each of the mixed baby greens. Place 4 or 5 shrimp around the rim of each glass. Insert 3 chive stems into the center. Place each glass on an individual serving plate and serve the cocktail sauce in a small bowl on the plate or spoon some of the sauce over the lettuce and shrimp. Garnish each plate with a lemon wedge. *Makes 4 first-course servings*

**Wine Pairing:** Sonoma County brut sparkling wine

65

## DUCK BREAST "PEPPER STEAK" WITH BRANDY AND GREEN PEPPERCORNS, CRISPY STONE GROUND GRITS, AND BRAISED GREENS WITH APPLES AND BACON

*This is a "Sonoma meets the Deep South" take on the traditional pepper steak. The brandy and green peppercorns are reminiscent of the classic French favorite, while the grits and greens remind you that the South can be a great source of inspiration for cooking almost anything.*

*We use naturally raised Liberty duck, which we buy from Jim Reichardt of Sonoma County Poultry in Penngrove. The gastrique—a reduction of caramelized sugar and blackberry vinegar—adds a sweet-and-sour, high-acid contrast to the fat in the duck; the polenta anchors the dish.*

## PAN-ROASTED SONOMA DUCK BREAST WITH MASCARPONE POLENTA AND BLACKBERRY GASTRIQUE

**LIBERTY DUCK**

*Jim Reichardt raises Sonoma County Poultry's Liberty brand ducks in Penngrove, north of Petaluma, and his flavorful fowl are served in top restaurants across the country. This fourth-generation farmer's Liberty ducks are related to Peking ducks, yet they have larger breasts and derive their flavor more from the flesh than the skin. Rich and meaty, Liberty duck has a subtle gamy note. "Our Liberty ducks are a strain of Peking duck that was developed in Denmark and is suited to a slower, less stressful style of rearing," Reichardt says. "This results in a market age of about nine weeks as opposed to six weeks for other commercially grown birds. Our temperate climate allows us to raise ducks year-round, on straw litter, in an open environment with a minimum of intrusion. They receive no antibiotics or hormones, and are fed a diet consisting largely of corn and other grains."*

# DUCK BREAST "PEPPER STEAK" WITH BRANDY AND GREEN PEPPERCORNS,

## CRISPY STONE GROUND GRITS, AND BRAISED GREENS WITH APPLES AND BACON

### Baked Grits

1¼ cups stone-ground grits
2 cups water
4 tablespoons unsalted butter
1½ cups heavy cream
1 teaspoon Tabasco sauce
1 teaspoon kosher salt

Freshly ground pepper to taste

### Braised Greens with Apples

4 slices bacon
3 Granny Smith apples, peeled, cored,
   and cut into ½-inch-thick slices
1 yellow onion, sliced
2 cloves garlic, sliced
¼ teaspoon red pepper flakes
3 cups water
½ cup apple cider or juice
2 tablespoons apple cider vinegar
2 bunches (about 1½ pounds) collard greens
   or kale, stemmed and chopped
Kosher salt and freshly ground pepper
   to taste

### Duck Breasts

2 Muscovy duck breasts (about 1½ pounds
   total), trimmed of excess fat
1½ teaspoons green peppercorns
½ cup brandy
1 cup chicken broth or stock
Kosher salt and freshly ground pepper
   to taste

For the grits: Butter four 1-cup ramekins. Pour the grits into a bowl and add cold water to cover. Whisk until the chaff comes to the top. Pour off the water and chaff. In a medium saucepan, combine the water, butter, and cream. Bring to a boil over medium-high heat. Add the Tabasco, salt, and pepper. Whisk in the grits and reduce the heat to low. Cook, stirring frequently, until thick and creamy, about 25 minutes. Spoon the grits equally into prepared ramekins, cover, and refrigerate for at least 1 hour or overnight.

For the braised greens: In a large, nonreactive saucepan, cook the bacon over medium-high heat until it has rendered most of its fat, 6 to 8 minutes. Stir in the apples, onions, garlic, and pepper flakes and cook until the onions soften, about 5 minutes. Add the water, apple cider, and vinegar and bring to a boil. Stir in the greens and reduce the heat to a simmer. Partially cover and cook, stirring occasionally, until very tender, about 1 hour.
Season with salt and pepper.

Score the skin of the duck breasts with a sharp knife in a diamond pattern. Season with salt and pepper. Lay the duck breasts, skin side down, in a large skillet. Set the pan over medium-low heat and cook until much of the fat has rendered, about 5 to 10 minutes. Drain the fat from the pan and increase the heat to medium. Cook until well browned,

about 5 minutes. Turn the duck breasts over and cook 6 to 8 minutes longer for medium-rare. Transfer the duck breasts to a plate and tent with aluminum foil to keep warm. Drain the excess fat from the pan and return to medium heat. Add the peppercorns. Remove the pan from the heat, well away from the flame, and carefully add the brandy and chicken broth. Return to medium heat, bring to a boil, and cook to reduce the sauce by half, about 5 minutes.

Meanwhile, preheat the oven to 400°F. Unmold the chilled grits, place on a baking sheet, and bake until heated through and crisp at the edges, 15 to 20 minutes. Place one cake on each of 4 plates and add one-fourth of the greens. Thinly slice the duck breasts across the grain, place slices on top of the greens, and drizzle with the sauce. Serve at once.
*Makes 4 main-course servings*

**Wine Pairing:** Russian River Valley Syrah or Dry Creek Zinfandel

# PAN-ROASTED SONOMA DUCK BREAST WITH

## MASCARPONE POLENTA AND BLACKBERRY GASTRIQUE

### Mascarpone Polenta

3 cups low-sodium chicken broth
1 cup heavy cream
¼ teaspoon salt
¾ cup polenta
¼ cup mascarpone cheese
2 tablespoons grated Parmesan cheese
1 tablespoon unsalted butter

### Duck Breasts

2 duck breasts, about 1½ pounds total,
   trimmed of excess fat
Kosher salt and freshly ground pepper
   to taste
1 teaspoon peanut oil

### Blackberry Gastrique

1 tablespoon sugar
¼ cup dry red wine
2 tablespoons blackberry vinegar
2 tablespoons cold unsalted butter, cut
   into small pieces
Kosher salt and freshly ground pepper
   to taste
½ cup fresh blackberries

For the polenta: In a medium saucepan, bring the broth, cream, and salt to a boil over medium-high heat. Gradually stir in the polenta in a thin stream. Reduce the heat to low and stir constantly until very thick and soft, 25 to 30 minutes. Stir in the mascarpone, Parmesan, and butter. Set aside and keep warm.

For the duck: Preheat the oven to 450°F. With a sharp knife, lightly score the duck skin in a diamond pattern and sprinkle with salt and pepper. Add the oil to a large ovenproof skillet and add the duck, skin side down. Place over high heat and cook, draining the fat periodically, until well browned, about 5 minutes. Turn and cook on the second side until lightly browned, 1 to 2 minutes. Turn the duck over again, transfer the pan to the oven, and roast for 8 to 10 minutes for medium-rare. Transfer to a plate (reserving the pan for the gastrique), tent with aluminum foil, and let rest for 10 minutes.

For the gastrique: Discard all but 2 teaspoons of the excess fat from the pan. Place the pan over medium-high heat and sprinkle in the sugar. Cook until caramelized, 1 to 2 minutes. Add the wine and vinegar and stir to scrape up the browned bits from the bottom of the pan. Cook to reduce by half, 2 to 3 minutes. Gradually whisk in the cold butter. Season with salt and pepper and stir in the blackberries. Remove from the heat and keep warm.

To serve, thinly slice the duck against the grain. Spoon a mound of polenta into the center of each of 4 serving plates. Top with duck slices and the blackberry gastrique, and serve. *Makes 4 main-course servings*

**Wine Pairing:** Carneros or Russian River Valley Pinot Noir

## GRILLED LAMB SIRLOIN WITH JALAPEÑO-MINT JELLY, GRILLED ASPARAGUS, AND PECAN RICE PILAF

*Lamb tastes great with sweet and hot flavors, as in Indian cooking where a spicy lamb dish is accompanied by a sweet fruit chutney. I have taken the tradition of pairing lamb with mint jelly and spiced it up by adding jalapeño chiles. The rice pilaf is a nice, light accompaniment.*

*Everything about this dish sings "spring." Green garlic, lamb, and asparagus are at their best in springtime. I use them frequently in my dishes at this time of year. Risotto takes more time to make than rice pilaf, but it's well worth the extra effort.*

**Lamb Sirloin Steaks**

4 lamb sirloin steaks, about 7 ounces each
1 teaspoon grated lemon zest
3 tablespoons fresh lemon juice
2 cloves garlic, crushed
2 teaspoons sweet Hungarian paprika
2 teaspoons dried oregano
1 teaspoon minced fresh rosemary
⅓ cup extra-virgin olive oil
2 teaspoons kosher salt
1 teaspoon freshly ground pepper

**Pecan Rice Pilaf**

1 cup chopped pecans
2 tablespoons unsalted butter
½ cup chopped yellow onion
½ cup chopped red bell pepper
2 green onions, thinly sliced
1⅓ cups long-grain rice
2 cups chicken stock or broth
1 bay leaf
½ teaspoon kosher salt

1 pound asparagus
1 tablespoon extra-virgin olive oil
Kosher salt and freshly ground pepper
   to taste
¼ cup fresh mint leaves, minced
1 cup (1 half-pint jar) jalapeño jelly
   (recipe follows)

Put the lamb steaks in a large baking dish. In a small bowl, stir the lemon zest and juice, garlic, paprika, oregano, rosemary, olive oil, salt, and pepper together. Pour over the lamb, cover, and refrigerate for at least 6 hours or overnight.

For the pilaf: Pour the pecans into a dry saucepan and toast over medium heat, stirring often, until lightly browned and fragrant, 2 minutes. Add the butter, onion, pepper, and green onions. Sauté until the onion is translucent, about 3 minutes.

Stir the rice into the pecan mixture. Stir in the chicken stock, bay leaf, and salt. Bring to a boil. Cover the pan, reduce the heat to low, and cook for 20 minutes. Remove from the heat and let stand for 5 minutes before uncovering. Remove the bay leaf and fluff the rice with a fork. Cover again and keep warm until ready to serve.

Prepare a medium-hot fire in a charcoal grill or preheat a gas grill to medium-high. Trim the tough bottom stalks from the asparagus and toss the stalks in a bowl with the olive oil, salt, and pepper. Grill the lamb for about 4 minutes on each side for medium-rare. Transfer to a platter, tent with aluminum foil, and let rest for 5 minutes. Place the asparagus on grill, perpendicular to the grill grids, and grill for 1 or 2 minutes on each side until lightly charred and tender. Transfer to a plate.

In a small serving bowl, stir the mint leaves into the jalapeño jelly. Divide the rice pilaf and asparagus evenly among 4 plates. Slice the lamb steaks and fan out each steak on the plates next to the asparagus and rice. Drizzle the jelly over the lamb and asparagus and pass the remaining jelly at the table. *Makes 4 main-course servings*

**Wine Pairing:** Sonoma County Merlot, Cabernet Sauvignon, or red Meritage

**Jalapeño Jelly**

2 jalapeño chiles, seeded and minced
1 red bell pepper, seeded, deribbed, and
   finely chopped
½ cup apple cider vinegar
2½ cups sugar
Pinch of salt
1½ ounces liquid pectin (half of a 3-ounce
   pouch)

In a medium nonreactive saucepan, combine the peppers, vinegar, sugar, and salt. Bring to a boil over medium-high heat. Stir in the liquid pectin and return to a full boil. Boil for 1 minute, stirring constantly and reducing the heat if needed to prevent the jelly from boiling over. Remove from the heat and let cool. Pour into 3 sterilized half-pint jars, cover, and refrigerate for at least 4 hours or up to 4 weeks. *Makes about 3 cups*

72

1 pound (1 large bunch) slender asparagus,
    trimmed
4 green onions, green parts only

4 cups chicken broth or stock
2 tablespoons extra-virgin olive oil
1 yellow onion, finely chopped
1 cup Arborio rice
⅓ cup dry white wine

1 tablespoon minced green garlic,
    or 2 cloves garlic, minced
3 tablespoons unsalted butter
¼ cup grated Parmigiano-Reggiano
    cheese, plus more for garnish
Kosher salt and freshly ground pepper
    to taste

### Grilled Lamb

4 lamb sirloin steaks, about 6 ounces each
Extra-virgin olive oil for coating
Kosher salt and freshly ground pepper
    to taste

In a large pot of salted boiling water, cook half of the asparagus (about 16 spears) until crisp-tender, 3 to 4 minutes. Using tongs, transfer to a cutting board and trim into 4-inch-long spears; reserve the stems. In the same pot, boil the remaining asparagus just until bright green, 2 minutes; remove with tongs and drain separately. Add the green onion tops to the boiling water and blanch for 15 seconds; drain.

Divide the trimmed spears into 4 equal bundles of about 4 spears each. Tie each bundle together with a green onion top and set aside. Cut the reserved stems and the remaining asparagus into ½-inch pieces and set aside for the risotto.

In a medium saucepan, bring the broth to a slow simmer. In a large skillet, heat the olive oil over medium-high heat and sauté the onion until translucent, about 3 minutes. Add the rice and cook, stirring, for 2 minutes. Add the wine and stir until absorbed. Add the hot broth, ½ cup at a time, stirring until each addition is absorbed, 20 to 25 minutes total. The rice should be al dente: firm but tender. Add the reserved asparagus, the green garlic, the butter, and the ¼ cup cheese and stir gently until combined, 2 minutes. Remove from the heat and season with salt and pepper. Set aside and cover to keep warm.

For the lamb: Prepare a medium fire in a charcoal grill, or preheat a gas grill to medium. Rub the lamb steaks with olive oil to coat and sprinkle with salt and pepper. Grill the lamb for about 4 minutes on each side for medium-rare. Transfer the lamb to a cutting board, tent loosely with aluminum foil, and let stand for 5 minutes.

Using a sharp knife, cut the steaks against the grain into thin diagonal slices. Place a row of slices on each of 4 plates. Stand a bundle of asparagus up next to each serving of lamb, and place a mound of risotto on the other side of the lamb slices. Sprinkle a little cheese on top of each risotto mound and serve. *Makes 4 main-course servings*

**Wine Pairing:** Sonoma Coast Pinot Noir or Alexander Valley Cabernet Franc

73

*Butterscotch is another old-fashioned flavor that I love. This crème brûlée was inspired by a butterscotch pudding I had a long time ago. We like to pair it with sweet anise-flavored cookies. The crisp texture of the cookies is a great accompaniment to the silky custard.*

*I like this homey dessert because it's cozy, comfortable, and richly satisfying. Who doesn't love butterscotch? I like to dress it up by serving it in an elegant glass topped with a swirl of soft and sexy whipped cream, an edible flower, a sprig of mint, and chocolate "cigarettes."*

2 tablespoons unsalted butter
2 cups heavy cream
¾ cup packed light brown sugar
½ vanilla bean, split lengthwise
¼ teaspoon kosher salt
6 large egg yolks
6 tablespoons granulated sugar

In a small saucepan, melt the butter over low heat. Stir in 1 cup of the cream and the brown sugar. Cook, stirring, until the sugar is completely dissolved. Scrape the seeds from the vanilla bean into the cream mixture. Add the pods, the remaining 1 cup cream, and the salt. Increase the heat to medium and bring to a boil; remove from the heat.

In a medium bowl, whisk the egg yolks to blend. Gradually whisk about one-third of the hot cream mixture into the egg yolks. Return to the pan, whisking to blending, then strain through a fine-mesh sieve into a bowl. Divide the custard among 6 crème brûlée dishes (4-ounce shallow ramekins). Place the dishes in a baking pan and carefully add hot water to come halfway up the sides of the ramekins. Bake until the centers of the custards jiggle when gently shaken, 30 to 35 minutes. Remove from oven and the water bath and let cool. Refrigerate for at least 2 hours or up to 24 hours.

Just before serving, evenly sprinkle each custard with 1 tablespoon of the granulated sugar. Using a kitchen blowtorch, caramelize the sugar until it is a deep mahogany color; do not allow to burn. Alternatively, place under a preheated broiler until the sugar is melted and browned, 2 to 3 minutes. Place each ramekin on a plate and serve. *Makes 6 servings*

**Wine Pairing:** Sonoma County late-harvest Gewürztraminer or Trosseau Gris

1 cup firmly packed dark brown sugar
⅓ cup cornstarch
½ teaspoon salt
2 cups milk
1½ cups heavy cream
4 tablespoons unsalted butter, cut into
    pieces
1 teaspoon vanilla extract
2 tablespoons purchased caramel sauce
Lightly sweetened whipped cream for
    serving
Chocolate cigarettes for garnish
    (available at specialty markets and
    grocery stores)

In a small bowl, combine the brown sugar, cornstarch, salt, and milk. Stir with a whisk to blend. In a saucepan, bring the cream to a boil over medium heat. Add the cornstarch mixture, butter, vanilla, and caramel sauce, and whisk constantly until the mixture returns to a boil, 4 to 5 minutes. Reduce the heat to a simmer and cook until very thick, 3 to 5 minutes longer. Remove from the heat, let cool slightly, and cover with plastic wrap pressed directly onto the surface. Refrigerate for at least 2 hours or up to 8 hours.

To serve, spoon into small bowls and top with a dollop of whipped cream. Add a couple of chocolate cigarettes if desired.
*Makes 6 to 8 servings*

**Wine Pairing:** Late-harvest Sauvignon Blanc

77

## DARK CHOCOLATE POUND CAKE
## WITH JUBILEE CHERRIES

*The recipe for cherries jubilee is more than one hundred years old.*
*The updated Zin version of this dessert poaches the first Bing cherries of*
*the season in brandy and serves them over a rich chocolate pound cake,*
*with a dollop of whipped cream on the side.*

*This is my enhanced version of molten chocolate cake. We bake and serve the cakes in coffee cups, with a creamer of cherry cream on the side, so that diners can add as much as they like. Chocolate and cherries are classic go-togethers in this not-too-sweet dessert.*

## WARM CHOCOLATE PUDDLE CAKES WITH CHERRY CREAM

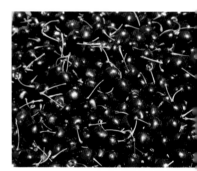

# DARK CHOCOLATE POUND CAKE WITH JUBILEE CHERRIES

## Chocolate Pound Cake

¾ cup miniature semisweet chocolate chips
1¾ cups all-purpose flour
½ cup plus 2 tablespoons unsweetened
  cocoa powder
½ teaspoon baking powder
½ teaspoon salt

¾ cup (1½ sticks) unsalted butter at room
  temperature
6 tablespoons nonhydrogenated vegetable
  shortening
1¾ cups sugar
3 large eggs
1 teaspoon vanilla extract
¾ cup whole milk

## Jubilee Cherries

1 cup sugar
2 tablespoons cornstarch
¼ teaspoon kosher salt
1½ cups water
2 pounds fresh Bing cherries, pitted
½ cup brandy
4 tablespoons unsalted butter

Lightly sweetened whipped cream for
  serving

For the chocolate pound cake: Preheat the oven to 325°F. Spray a 9-by-5-inch loaf pan with cooking oil spray.

In a small bowl, combine the chocolate chips with ¼ cup of the flour and the 2 tablespoons cocoa powder. Stir with a whisk to blend. In a medium bowl, combine the remaining 1½ cups flour and the ½ cup cocoa powder, the baking powder, and salt. Stir with a whisk to blend. Set both bowls aside.

Using an electric mixer on medium speed, beat the butter, shortening, and sugar together until light and fluffy. Add the eggs one at a time, beating well after each addition. Beat in the vanilla extract.

With the electric mixer on low speed, alternately add the flour mixture and the milk to the butter mixture in three additions. Stir in the chocolate chip mixture until blended.

Pour the batter into the prepared pan and bake until a toothpick inserted in the center of the cake comes out clean, about 1½ hours. Let cool completely on a wire rack. Run a knife around the sides of the pan and unmold the cake onto the rack.

For the jubilee cherries: In a medium saucepan, combine the sugar, cornstarch, salt, and water. Cook over low heat, stirring until the sugar has dissolved. Add the cherries, increase the heat to medium, and cook until the syrup has thickened, about 15 minutes. Remove from the heat and stir in the brandy. Return to low heat and cook another 5 minutes. Whisk in the butter 1 tablespoon at a time and remove from the heat.

Cut the cake into slices and place a slice on each of 8 dessert plates. Top each slice with a dollop of whipped cream and ladle the warm cherries and syrup over all. *Makes 8 servings*

**Wine Pairing:** Dry Creek Valley late-harvest Zinfandel

# WARM CHOCOLATE PUDDLE CAKES WITH CHERRY CREAM

½ cup (1 stick) plus 6 tablespoons unsalted butter
3 ounces bittersweet chocolate, chopped
½ cup unsweetened cocoa powder
1 cup sugar
3 large eggs
2 teaspoons vanilla extract
⅓ cup mascarpone cheese at room temperature
½ cup all-purpose flour
Pinch of salt

## Cherry Cream

1 cup fresh cherries, pitted (or frozen cherries, thawed and drained, if fresh are unavailable)
1 tablespoon Kirschwasser (cherry brandy), optional
1½ cups heavy cream
Pinch of salt

Preheat the oven to 325°F and butter six 6-ounce coffee cups or ramekins. In a small saucepan, melt the butter and chocolate over medium-low heat until smooth. Remove from the heat, pour into a bowl, and whisk in the cocoa, then the sugar, until smooth. Using an electric mixer on medium speed, beat in the eggs and vanilla until smooth. Beat in the mascarpone until smooth. Stir in the flour and salt until blended, scraping down the sides of the bowl as needed.

Divide the batter among the prepared cups or ramekins and bake until the cakes are set around the edges but still liquid in the center, 10 to 15 minutes; do not overbake. Let cool 2 to 3 minutes.

To make the cherry cream: In a blender, combine the cherries and brandy, if using. Blend until smooth. Add the cream and salt and pulse until well combined and slightly thickened. Use at once, or cover and chill for up to 12 hours. *Makes about 3 cups*

To serve, place the puddle cakes onto individual dessert plates. Pour 4 tablespoons of cherry cream over each cake or serve in small pitchers on the side. *Makes 6 servings*

**Wine Pairing:** Late-harvest Zinfandel or other port-style red wine

*As wine grapes make their preharvest push toward ripeness, gardens and orchards explode with wave after wave of peak-of-season vegetables, fruits, fresh herbs, and edible flowers.*

The promise of spring is kept in summer, when everything seemingly ripens at once: berries, cherries, figs, melons, peaches, plums, corn, peppers, tomatoes, squashes, basil, and, in late summer, wine grapes. Farmers' markets offer crayon-box palettes of just-picked produce, some of it still warm from the sun. Chefs' menus change daily to take advantage of what's freshest at any given moment. Summer is grilling season, so Pacific wild king salmon and juicy beefsteaks are seared and enjoyed by themselves, or as components in more complex dishes. Sweet corn, peppers and chiles, blackberries, and peaches are at their very best, yet if you ask chefs to name their no. 1 ingredient of summer, it's the heirloom tomato, with hundreds of varieties grown in wine country, in all colors, shapes, sizes, and flavors. Meanwhile, the grape harvest typically begins in early September.

*Sliced summer tomatoes with fresh basil, fried green tomatoes with "el rancho" dressing, and sautéed cherry tomatoes with good bacon: If you're crazy about tomatoes, like me, this is the ultimate summer dish. The different textures and temperatures make this salad unique.*

### DAVERO SONOMA

86   *Every luscious tomato salad deserves a high-quality olive oil, which is why Ridgely Evers and Colleen McGlynn started their own olive oil company in Dry Creek Valley. Evers, a former executive at Intuit, and McGlynn, the chef-owner of a former restaurant in Healdsburg, were well ahead of the U.S. artisan movement in extra-virgin olive oil production, taking cuttings from an old olive grove in Tuscany in 1988 and planting them on their Olive Ridge Ranch. By 1997, DaVero was the first American extra-virgin olive oil to win a blind tasting in Italy, and it found wide favor with chefs. From forty-five hundred trees, DaVero produces olio nuovo ("new oil" pressed right after harvest), estate extra-virgin and Meyer lemon olive oils, and a multipurpose 30-Weight Utility Olive Oil and Line Lube, created for restaurant line cooks.*

*Sonoma County is blessed with an amazing array of tomatoes. When they're at their peak of juicy ripeness, we call on Dan Magnuson of Soda Rock Farm for some of the forty heirloom varieties he grows in the Alexander and Dry Creek Valleys. When we can no longer get ripe local tomatoes, this dish comes off the menu.*

## HEIRLOOM TOMATO SALAD WITH YELLOW TOMATO VINAIGRETTE, BASIL OIL, AND BURRATA CHEESE

### SODA ROCK FARM

*Dan Magnuson is "the man" when it comes to supplying just-picked tomatoes to local restaurants. Terrific tomatoes are grown throughout wine country, yet Dan's forty varieties of beef-steak and heirloom tomatoes, cultivated on his two farms, have that extra bit of flavor and a healthier glow than most other tomatoes, thanks to plenty of sunlight, rich soils, mango mulch, ground oyster shells, and ten years of trial and error. Dan grew up in the Alexander Valley, studied horticulture in college, became a tennis pro, and still teaches the sport in Santa Rosa. His tomatoes are sold in some grocery stores and at several Northern California farmers' markets, yet the core of Magnuson's business is sales to restaurants.*

### El Rancho Dressing

¼ cup mayonnaise
¼ cup sour cream
2 tablespoons pickled jalapeño juice
    (from 1 small can pickled jalapeños)
1½ teaspoons red wine vinegar
½ teaspoon fresh lemon juice
½ teaspoon dry mustard, such as Colman's
½ teaspoon sweet Hungarian paprika
½ teaspoon kosher salt
¼ teaspoon onion powder
¼ teaspoon dill seed, crushed
⅛ teaspoon celery seed
Freshly ground pepper to taste

### Sliced Summer Tomatoes

1 pound tomatoes of varying colors,
    sliced ½ inch thick
½ cup loosely packed fresh basil leaves
Salt and freshly ground pepper to taste

### Fried Green Tomatoes

3 tablespoons cornmeal
3 tablespoons masa harina
    (Mexican corn flour )
Salt and freshly ground pepper to taste
8 ounces green (unripe) tomatoes,
    sliced ½ inch thick
¼ cup all-purpose flour
1 large egg, beaten
Canola oil for frying

### Cherry Tomato Sauté

2 tablespoons minced fresh basil
1 tablespoon red wine vinegar
¼ cup extra-virgin olive oil
8 slices bacon, diced
1 pint cherry tomatoes, stemmed
    and halved
Salt and freshly ground pepper to taste

For the el rancho dressing: In a small bowl, combine all the ingredients and stir with a whisk to blend. Set aside.

For the sliced tomatoes: Layer the tomato slices with the basil leaves on one-third of a platter. Sprinkle with salt and pepper. (Alternatively, arrange the tomatoes on 4 individual plates.)

For the fried green tomatoes: In a shallow bowl, combine the cornmeal, masa harina, salt, and pepper. Stir with a whisk to blend. Dredge the green tomato slices in the flour, shaking off the excess, then dip in the egg, letting excess drip off. Turn the slices in the cornmeal mixture to coat evenly. In a large cast-iron skillet, heat ¼ inch oil over medium-high heat until it shimmers. Working in batches, add the coated tomatoes and fry for about 2 minutes on each side, or until golden brown. Arrange the slices on the platter next to the sliced summer tomatoes.

For the cherry tomato sauté: In a small bowl, combine the basil, vinegar, and olive oil; whisk to blend. In a medium skillet, cook the bacon over medium heat, stirring, until mostly crisp, about 7 minutes. Remove from the heat and drain off the fat. Return to the heat, add the cherry tomatoes, and cook until heated through, 1 minute. Add the basil vinaigrette, salt, and pepper. Remove from the heat.

Spoon the cherry tomato sauté alongside the fried green tomatoes. Drizzle the fried green tomatoes with the el rancho dressing and serve. *Makes 4 first-course servings*

**Wine Pairing:** Russian River Valley Sauvignon Blanc

**Yellow Tomato Vinaigrette**
¼ cup extra-virgin olive oil
1 tablespoon rice wine vinegar
½ small yellow tomato, peeled, seeded,
    and chopped (about ¼ cup)
1 teaspoon minced shallot
Kosher salt and freshly ground pepper
    to taste

**Basil Oil**
1 cup fresh basil leaves, plus 4 small
    sprigs for garnish
¼ cup canola oil

2 pounds ripe multicolored heirloom
    tomatoes, cut into ¼-inch-thick
    crosswise slices
4 ounces burrata or fresh mozzarella cheese
    (see Note)
Balsamic vinegar for drizzling

For the tomato vinaigrette: In a blender,
combine all the ingredients and process
until smooth.

For the basil oil: In a medium pot of salted
boiling water, blanch the basil for 20 seconds.
Immediately drain and transfer to a bowl
of ice water. Squeeze the leaves dry and
chop coarsely. In the blender, combine the
chopped basil and canola oil and blend until
smooth. Pour through a fine-mesh sieve
into a small bowl.

Arrange the tomato slices on 4 salad plates.
Top each with a thick slice of burrata cheese.
Top the burrata with a sprig of basil. Drizzle
the basil oil, balsamic vinegar, and a little of
the yellow tomato vinaigrette around each
salad and serve. *Makes 4 first-course
servings*

**Wine Pairing:** Sonoma County Sauvignon
Blanc

Note: Burrata is a creamy Italian cow's-milk
cheese crafted from fresh mozzarella curds.
It can be found in specialty cheese shops
and should be refrigerated and consumed
within a few days of purchase.

89

## CHILLED MELON SOUP
## WITH JALAPEÑOS AND MINT

*This is a soup for the long, hot days of August when the local melons are at their peak of sweetness. Fire and ice, sweet and sour, hot and cold all describe this simple, refreshing treat. Garnish each serving with a dollop of crème fraîche and a sprig of summer mint.*

90

*Light and easy to prepare, this summer soup is ideal on a hot day. The combination of cold, sweet, and spice is utterly refreshing, and I love to see the reactions of people who taste it for the first time; the spiciness comes as a pleasant surprise.*

2 teaspoons olive oil

1 jalapeño chile, seeded and minced

1 ripe cantaloupe or honeydew melon
(about 2½ pounds), halved and seeded

1 cup buttermilk

¼ cup seasoned rice wine vinegar, plus
more to taste

1 cup loosely packed fresh mint leaves, plus
a few sprigs for garnish

2 teaspoons kosher salt

About ¼ cup crème fraîche for serving

In a small skillet, heat the oil over medium-high heat. Add the jalapeño and cook, stirring, for 1 minute. Remove from the heat and set aside.

Scoop out the flesh of the melon and cut it into small chunks. Working in batches if necessary, put the melon chunks in a blender with the buttermilk, the ¼ cup rice wine vinegar, the mint, and salt. Puree until smooth. Add the jalapeño and pulse to mix. Taste and add more vinegar as desired (up to ¼ cup, depending on the sweetness of the melon).

Refrigerate for at least 1 hour or up to 24 hours; whisk to recombine before serving. To serve, ladle into shallow bowls and dollop with the crème fraîche. *Makes 4 first-course servings*

**Wine Pairing:** Alexander Valley or Dry Creek Valley Sauvignon Blanc

1 teaspoon pasilla chile powder
1 teaspoon pimentón (Spanish smoked
    paprika)
1 teaspoon New Mexico chile powder
½ cup sugar
½ cup water
1 small seedless watermelon (about
    3½ pounds), peeled and cut into chunks
½ red onion, finely chopped
1 red bell pepper, seeded, deribbed, and
    finely chopped
1 yellow bell pepper, seeded, deribbed,
    and finely chopped
¼ cup finely chopped fresh cilantro, plus
    sprigs for garnish
2 limes, plus 1 more if needed
Salt and freshly ground pepper to taste
1 ripe avocado, peeled, pitted, and sliced,
    for garnish

In a small dry skillet, combine the chile powder, pimentón, and New Mexico chile powder. Stir over medium heat until lightly toasted and fragrant, 1 to 2 minutes.

In a small pan, combine the sugar and water. Stir over medium heat until the sugar has dissolved; bring to a boil. Remove from the heat and let cool.

Put half of the watermelon in a blender and add ¼ cup of the sugar syrup. Blend until smooth. Set aside. Finely chop the remaining watermelon and put in a medium bowl with the onion, peppers, cilantro, and toasted spices. Grate in the zest of 1 lime. Add the watermelon puree and the juice of 2 limes; taste and add more if needed to balance the flavors. Season with salt and pepper. Refrigerate for at least 1 hour or up to 24 hours.

To serve, spoon into small bowls or glasses. Garnish each serving with cilantro sprigs, avocado slices, and a slice of lime and serve.
*Makes 6 first-course servings*

**Wine Pairing:** Chilled dry rosé of Syrah or Grenache, or Pinot Noir

93

## BACON-WRAPPED WILD KING SALMON ON SWEET CORN GRITS WITH ROASTED TOMATO BROTH AND ARUGULA-BASIL SALAD

*Somebody once said, "Everything tastes better with bacon." I am in full agreement, and salmon is no exception. This is a "summer's greatest hits" recipe featuring wild salmon—available to us from May through October— along with tomatoes, corn, and basil.*

94

*When local king salmon is running, I buy all I can until the season is over. We serve only wild salmon, not farm-raised, because when it comes to taste and texture, wild salmon is superior, and it's better for you and the environment. The sweetness of fresh summer corn perfectly complements the richness of the salmon.*

### Grits

Kernels cut from 2 ears white corn
3 cups water
¼ cup heavy cream, plus more as needed
2 tablespoons unsalted butter
¼ teaspoon Tabasco sauce
1 cup stone-ground grits
Salt and freshly ground pepper to taste

### Salmon Fillets

4 wild king salmon fillets (about 6 ounces
    each), skin and pin bones removed
Salt and freshly ground pepper to taste
4 slices bacon
1 tablespoon olive oil

### Arugula-Basil Salad

2 cups loosely packed baby arugula leaves
1 cup loosely packed small fresh basil leaves
1 tablespoon extra-virgin olive oil
1 teaspoon red wine vinegar
Kosher salt and freshly ground pepper
    to taste

Roasted Tomato Broth for drizzling
    (recipe follows)

For the grits: In a small saucepan, bring 1 inch water to a boil over high heat. Add the corn kernels and cook just until tender, 2 minutes. Drain and set aside. In a medium saucepan, bring the water, the ¼ cup cream, the butter, and Tabasco sauce to a boil over medium-high heat. Gradually whisk in the grits in a slow, steady stream. Reduce the heat to low and cook, stirring occasionally, until very thick and creamy, about 40 minutes; if too thick, stir in a little more cream to thin. Stir in the corn kernels and season with salt and pepper.

For the salmon fillets: Preheat the oven to 400°F. Sprinkle the salmon with salt and pepper. Wrap each fillet around the center with a slice of bacon and secure with a toothpick. In a large ovenproof skillet, heat the olive oil over medium-high heat. Add the fillets and cook for 2 minutes on each side, or until the bacon is lightly browned and beginning to crisp. Transfer the skillet to the oven and bake the salmon for 5 to 7 minutes for medium-rare. Remove from the oven and remove the toothpicks. Set aside and keep warm.

For the salad: In a medium bowl, whisk together the olive oil and vinegar, and season with salt and pepper. Add the arugula and basil leaves and toss well.

To serve, divide the grits among 4 rimmed plates or shallow bowls. Drizzle each with ¼ cup of the tomato broth (save the remaining broth for other uses), top each with a salmon fillet, and garnish with the salad. *Makes 4 main-course servings*

**Wine Pairing:** Sonoma County Chardonnay or Sangiovese

### Roasted Tomato Broth

6 Roma tomatoes, halved lengthwise
1 yellow onion
1 tablespoon olive oil
Salt and freshly ground pepper to taste
3 cups water

Preheat the oven to 400°F. In a medium bowl, toss the tomatoes and onion with the olive oil and sprinkle with salt and pepper. Place in a roasting pan cut sides up and bake until the tomato skins are blackened, 15 to 20 minutes. Transfer the tomatoes and onion to a medium saucepan and add the water. Bring to a boil over high heat, reduce the heat to maintain a simmer, and cook for 30 minutes. Remove from the heat and let cool slightly, then puree in a blender. Strain through a fine-mesh sieve. Taste and adjust the seasoning. Use now or rewarm over low heat. Store covered in the refrigerator for up to 3 days. *Makes about 3 cups*

**Panzanella Dressing**

2 tablespoons balsamic vinegar

1 clove garlic, minced

1 tablespoon minced shallot

¼ cup extra-virgin olive oil

Salt and freshly ground pepper to taste

**Panzanella**

2 cups country-style bread, torn into
  1-inch chunks

1 tablespoon extra-virgin olive oil

2 cups arugula

1 cup diced heirloom tomatoes

¼ cup thinly sliced red onion

½ cup diced cucumber

2 cups corn kernels (from about 3 ears
  of corn)

**Salmon**

4 fillets (6 ounces each) wild Pacific salmon,
  pin bones removed

2 tablespoons extra-virgin olive oil, plus
  more for drizzling

Kosher salt and freshly ground pepper
  to taste

For the dressing: In a small bowl, whisk the vinegar, garlic, and shallot together. Gradually whisk in the olive oil until combined. Season with salt and pepper.

For the panzanella: Preheat the oven to 350°F. In a medium bowl, toss the bread with the olive oil and spread on a rimmed baking sheet. Bake, stirring occasionally, until golden brown, 8 to 10 minutes. Remove from the oven and let cool. In a large bowl, toss the bread cubes with the arugula, tomatoes, onion, cucumber, and corn kernels. Drizzle in the panzanella dressing and toss to coat.

For the salmon, prepare a medium-hot fire in a charcoal grill or preheat a gas grill to medium-high heat. Oil the grill grids. Brush the salmon with the 2 tablespoons olive oil and season with salt and pepper. Place the salmon on the grill, skin side up, and cook until grill-marked, about 5 minutes. Carefully turn over and cook 4 to 6 minutes longer for medium-rare.

To serve, mound the salad on plates and top with the salmon filets. Drizzle with additional olive oil and the vin cotto and serve. *Makes 4 main-course servings*

**Wine Pairing:** Sonoma County Chardonnay

97

## GRILLED RIB-EYE "RANCHERO," SUMMER SQUASH "CALABACITAS," GRILLED SCALLIONS, AND WARM TORTILLAS

*The Las Flores Café in my hometown of Newman, California, serves a rib-eye steak in a spicy Mexican red sauce. My parents started bringing me there right after I was born. It's still my favorite place to go when I'm home. This is my version of the Las Flores dish.*

*I love the flavor of a thick, meaty steak topped with earthy truffle butter—richness times two. Yet the dish is not overwhelming, thanks to the acidity in the refreshing watercress salad. For the best result, prepare the truffle butter with fresh black truffle, though truffle oil works nicely, too.*

**GRILLED RIB-EYE STEAK WITH BLACK TRUFFLE BUTTER, WATERCRESS SALAD, AND SALT-ROASTED POTATOES**

## GRILLED RIB-EYE "RANCHERO," SUMMER SQUASH "CALABACITAS,"
## GRILLED SCALLIONS, AND WARM TORTILLAS

**Ranchero Sauce**

1 teaspoon cumin seeds
2 pounds ripe tomatoes
½ yellow onion, sliced
2 poblano chiles, seeded and deribbed
1 red bell pepper, seeded and deribbed
2 peeled garlic cloves
1 tablespoon olive oil
2 teaspoons dried oregano, preferably
  Mexican
2 cups chicken broth or stock
2 teaspoons red wine vinegar
Salt and freshly ground pepper to taste

**Summer Squash**

2 ears corn, husked
4 tablespoons unsalted butter
1 yellow onion, chopped
1 Anaheim chile, seeded, deribbed, and
  chopped
2 pounds summer squash, cut into
  small dice
½ cup heavy cream
Salt and freshly ground pepper to taste

4 rib-eye steaks (10 ounces each)
Salt and freshly ground pepper to taste
4 green onions
1 tablespoon olive oil
Warm flour tortillas for serving

For the ranchero sauce: Preheat the oven to 450°F. In a small dry skillet over medium heat, stir the cumin seeds until fragrant, 1 to 2 minutes. Grind in a spice grinder or clean coffee grinder. Set aside.

In a large bowl, toss the tomatoes, onion, poblano chiles, bell pepper, and garlic cloves with the olive oil. Spread in a single layer in a roasting pan and bake until the vegetables are blackened in spots, 15 to 20 minutes. Remove from the oven.

Transfer the vegetables to a large saucepan. Add the cumin, oregano, and broth. Bring to a boil. Reduce to a simmer and cook for 20 minutes. Working in batches, puree in a blender, then strain through a fine-mesh sieve into a bowl. Stir in the red wine vinegar, and season with salt and pepper. Serve now, or reheat over low heat. Store covered in the refrigerator for up to 3 days or in the freezer for up to 1 month. *Makes about 1 quart*

For the summer squash: In a large pot of boiling water, cook the corn until just tender, 2 minutes; immediately plunge into ice water to stop the cooking. Drain and cut the kernels from the cobs.

In a large skillet, melt the butter over medium heat. Add the onion and chile and cook, stirring, until the onion is translucent, 3 to 4 minutes. Add the squash and cook for 2 minutes. Add the corn kernels and cook for 1 minute more. Add the cream, bring to a boil, and cook until cream has thickened, about 5 minutes. Season with salt and pepper. Set aside and keep warm, or reheat just before serving.

Prepare a medium-hot fire in a charcoal grill or preheat a gas grill to medium-high. Oil the grill grids. Season the steaks with salt and pepper and grill for 4 to 5 minutes on each side for medium-rare. Transfer to a plate, tent with foil, and let rest for 5 minutes. Meanwhile, toss the green onions in the olive oil and season with salt and pepper to taste. Grill until well marked, about 30 seconds on each side.

Divide the squash among 4 plates. Slice the steaks and fan slices on each plate. Drizzle with the ranchero sauce and top with the green onions. Pass additional sauce and the warm tortillas at the table. *Makes 4 main-course servings*

**Wine Pairing:** Sonoma County Sangiovese, Tempranillo, or Zinfandel

100

## GRILLED RIB-EYE STEAK WITH BLACK TRUFFLE BUTTER, WATERCRESS SALAD,

## AND SALT-ROASTED POTATOES

**Black Truffle Butter**

1 fresh black truffle, or 6 to 8 drops black truffle oil
½ cup unsalted European high-fat butter at room temperature
Salt to taste

**Salt-Roasted Potatoes**

8 small Yukon Gold potatoes (about 1 pound total)
3 to 4 cups kosher salt

**Grilled Steaks**

4 rib-eye steaks (10 ounces each)
Kosher salt and freshly ground pepper to taste

**Watercress Salad**

1 tablespoon minced shallot
1 teaspoon Dijon mustard
1 tablespoon red wine vinegar
2 tablespoons extra-virgin olive oil
4 cups loosely packed watercress leaves (about 2 bunches)

Fleur de sel for sprinkling

For the black truffle butter: Using a small, sharp knife, or vegetable peeler, shave the truffle over the butter in a small bowl. Stir well to blend; stir in the salt. Or, stir the truffle oil and salt into the butter to blend. Shape into a log, wrap in plastic wrap, and refrigerate for at least 2 hours or overnight.

For the salt-roasted potatoes: Preheat the oven to 350°F. Put the potatoes in a baking dish, spacing them about 1 inch apart. Cover completely with the kosher salt. Bake until tender, about 1 hour. Thoroughly brush off the salt. Set aside and keep warm.

For the steaks, prepare a hot fire in a charcoal grill, or preheat a gas grill to high. Oil the grill grids. Season the steaks well with salt and pepper. Grill for 4 to 5 minutes on each side for medium-rare. Transfer to a plate, tent loosely with aluminum foil, and let rest for 10 minutes.

For the watercress salad: In a small bowl, whisk the shallot, mustard, and vinegar together. Gradually whisk in the olive oil. Pour over the watercress leaves in a large bowl and toss to coat.

To serve, place a steak on each of 4 plates. Sprinkle each steak with fleur de sel. Cut the truffle butter into thick slices and place 1 slice on top of each steak. Arrange 2 potatoes and some watercress salad alongside each steak, and serve. *Makes 4 main-course servings*

**Wine Pairing:** Alexander Valley, Sonoma Valley, or Dry Creek Valley Cabernet Sauvignon

## TOASTED MASA AND CORNMEAL SHORTCAKES
## WITH FRESH BERRIES AND CREMA

*I love the Southwestern flavor that masa harina gives to these cornmeal shortcakes. Toasting the shortcakes just before serving gives this dessert a nice contrast in temperatures and textures. Top with whatever berries are sweetest and in season.*

## MIXED BERRY TRIFLE WITH MEYER LEMON CURD

*Lemon curd, combined with whipped cream and fresh local berries, takes the classic trifle to a higher level. Meyer lemons, which grow in the yards of many Sonoma residents, yield a sweeter, richer juice, along with a lemony tang. If you prefer, make one large trifle in a glass bowl and spoon out servings.*

### Masa Shortcakes

1 cup all-purpose flour
¼ cup stone-ground cornmeal
2 tablespoons masa harina
    (Mexican corn flour)
2 tablespoons sugar, plus more for
    sprinkling
1 tablespoon baking powder
½ teaspoon kosher salt
1½ teaspoons grated lemon zest
5 tablespoons cold unsalted butter,
    cut into chunks
½ cup heavy cream, plus more for
    brushing

### Topping

½ cup sour cream
2 tablespoons fresh lemon juice
4 tablespoons sugar
2 cups mixed fresh berries (such as
    sliced strawberries, blueberries,
    and blackberries)

For the shortcakes: Preheat the oven to 350°F. In a food processor, combine the flour, cornmeal, masa harina, the 2 tablespoons sugar, baking powder, salt, and lemon zest. Pulse to blend. Add the butter and pulse until the mixture resembles coarse crumbs. With the machine running, add the ½ cup cream and process just until combined. Turn the dough out onto a lightly floured board and knead gently a few times to form a smooth ball.

With a floured rolling pin, roll the dough into a ¾-inch-thick round. Using a 2½-inch round biscuit cutter, cut out 4 rounds (gathering and rerolling scraps as needed), pressing straight down without twisting the cutter. Place on a baking sheet; brush the tops with cream and sprinkle with sugar. Bake until golden brown and well risen, about 25 minutes. Remove from the oven and transfer to a wire rack to cool.

For the topping: In a small bowl, whisk together the sour cream, lemon juice, and 2 tablespoons of the sugar. In another bowl, toss the berries with the remaining 2 tablespoons sugar.

To serve, preheat the broiler. Split the cooled shortcakes in half and lightly toast, split side up, under the broiler for 1 minute, or until very lightly browned. Place a short-cake bottom on each of 4 dessert plates. Dollop each with the sour cream mixture, spoon the berry mixture over, and top with the top half of a shortcake. Serve at once.
*Makes 4 servings*

**Wine Pairing:** Late-harvest Chardonnay or other white dessert wine

**Sponge Cake**
1½ cups all-purpose flour
1½ teaspoons baking powder
Pinch of salt
5 large eggs, separated
1¼ cups sugar
⅓ cup boiling water
1 teaspoon pure vanilla extract

**Simple Syrup**
1 cup sugar
1 cup water
1 tablespoon Grand Marnier

**Meyer Lemon Curd**
3 large eggs
6 large egg yolks
¾ cup sugar
¼ teaspoon salt
Grated zest of 2 Meyer lemons
½ cup plus 2 tablespoons fresh Meyer
   lemon juice
6 tablespoons unsalted butter, cut into
   chunks

2 cups mixed fresh berries (such as
   raspberry, blueberry, and blackberry),
   plus more for garnish
1 tablespoon Grand Marnier
1 cup heavy cream
Fresh mint leaves for garnish
2 teaspoons confectioners' sugar

For the sponge cake: Preheat the oven to 350°F. Line an 11½-by-17½-inch jelly roll pan with parchment paper and butter the paper and the sides of the pan.

Sift together the flour, baking powder, and salt. Using an electric mixer, beat the egg yolks and sugar on high speed until thick and pale yellow. Reduce to medium speed and gradually add the boiling water and the vanilla. Scrape the sides and bottom of the bowl. Return the mixer to high speed and continue beating for about 5 minutes, until the mixture is again thick and ribbony. Gradually fold the flour mixture into the egg mixture until blended.

In another bowl, with clean beaters, beat the egg whites on high speed until soft peaks form. Fold half of the whipped whites into the batter, then fold in the remaining whites until no white streaks remain. Spread the batter evenly in the prepared pan.

Bake the cake until the top is golden brown and springs back when lightly pressed, 15 to 18 minutes. Remove from the oven and let cool.

For the simple syrup: In a small saucepan, combine the sugar and water. Bring to a boil, stirring until the sugar is dissolved. Remove from the heat and let cool to room temperature. Stir in the Grand Marnier and set aside.

For the lemon curd: In a heatproof bowl set over (not touching) simmering water in a saucepan, combine the eggs, egg yolks, sugar, salt, and lemon zest and juice. Whisking constantly, cook until thick, about 15 minutes. Remove from the heat and gradually whisk in the butter. Pour through a fine-mesh sieve into a bowl and let cool completely. Cover and refrigerate until ready to use.

To assemble the trifles, combine the 2 cups berries and Grand Marnier in a small bowl. In a deep bowl, whip the cream until soft peaks form. Cut out 8 rounds from the sponge cake using a small round biscuit cutter that fits the size of your serving glasses. Brush each round with the simple syrup. In 4 parfait or tall dessert glasses, layer the lemon curd, cake rounds, berries, and whipped cream. Top each trifle with a few berries and a sprig of mint, and place the glass on a dessert plate. Dust the plates with confectioners' sugar and serve. *Makes 4 servings*

**Wine Pairing:** Sonoma County sweet Muscat

105

## WARM PEACH TURNOVERS WITH VANILLA BEAN ICE CREAM

*Two of the best things about summer are ripe peaches and homemade ice cream. If you don't have time to make your own ice cream, look for a quality store-bought brand.*

### DRY CREEK PEACH & PRODUCE

*The fruit orchards that once dotted the Dry Creek Valley landscape near Healdsburg have been replaced by more profitable grapevines, except for one: Dry Creek Peach & Produce. Brian Sullivan and Gayle Okumura Sullivan, owners of the fifty-year-old farm since 2000, have remained steadfast in their commitment to growing organic yellow and white peaches, nectarines, and plums that are tree-ripened, hand-picked, and hand-packed—perhaps the sweetest, juiciest stone fruits you'll ever taste. Peach season runs June through September, and during the summer, Dry Creek Peach & Produce (so named because the Sullivans also grow tomatoes and Walla Walla onions) operates a farm stand on weekends and sells at Sonoma County gourmet grocery stores and farmers' markets.*

*The barbecue grill isn't just for meat, fish, and vegetables. Use it to grill fresh fruit for desserts—and no fruit takes better to a grill than fresh peaches. Grilling caramelizes the natural sugars in the peaches, and the honey-rosemary sauce adds a sweet and savory complement.*

## GRILLED PEACHES WITH HONEY-ROSEMARY SAUCE AND VANILLA ICE CREAM

### HECTOR'S HONEY FARM

Hector Alvarez, a third-generation beekeeper who learned the business from his grandfather in Mexico, supervises hives throughout wine country, with a base in Fulton, a tiny town north of Santa Rosa. He worked with his father in Sebastopol apple orchards, collecting bee swarms and transferring them to his hives. When his father returned to Mexico, Hector turned to the Sonoma County Beekeepers Club for advice, and soon began selling his honey. The business has expanded to include renting his bees to farms, so that the insects can pollinate other crops, such as almonds, apples, pears, and melons. Bees are prone to disease and sensitive to chemicals, so Alvarez places his hives in areas free from spraying. Hector and his wife, Susan, also make bee pollen and beeswax candles, which they sell at farmers' markets.

**Vanilla Bean Ice Cream**
7 large egg yolks
1 cup sugar
Pinch of salt
1 cup whole milk
2½ cups heavy cream
1 vanilla bean, split lengthwise

2 to 3 ripe peaches (1 pound total), plus
    1 more for garnish
¼ cup sugar, plus more for sprinkling
2 tablespoons cornstarch
1 tablespoon fresh lemon juice
⅛ teaspoon ground cinnamon
⅛ teaspoon freshly ground nutmeg
Pinch of salt
One 10-inch square sheet frozen puff pastry
    (half of a 17-ounce package), thawed
1 large egg, beaten

For the ice cream: In a medium bowl, whisk the egg yolks with the sugar and salt until pale and thick. Set aside. In a large saucepan, combine the milk and cream. Scrape the seeds from the vanilla bean into the milk mixture and add the pods. Bring to a simmer over medium heat.

Gradually whisk about 1 cup of the cream mixture into the egg-yolk mixture. Return to the pan and cook, stirring constantly, until the mixture thickens enough to coat the back of a spoon, 4 to 6 minutes. Strain through a fine-mesh sieve into a large bowl (reserve the pods for other uses) and let cool. Cover and refrigerate for at least 6 hours or up to 24 hours.

Freeze in an ice-cream maker according to manufacturer's instructions. Serve softly frozen, or cover and freeze until firm, up to 3 days.

Preheat the oven to 375°F and line a baking sheet with parchment paper. Cut a small X in the skin of each peach and blanch in a large pot of boiling water for 20 seconds. Plunge into ice water to stop the cooking, then pull off the skins. Halve, pit, and cut 2 of the peaches into ½-inch-thick slices (reserve the third peach for garnish). In a medium bowl, combine the peach slices, the ¼ cup sugar, the cornstarch, lemon juice, cinnamon, nutmeg, and salt. Toss to coat the peaches.

Carefully unfold the puff pastry square on a work surface and, with a large, sharp knife, cut it into four 5-inch squares. Lay the puff pastry squares on the prepared baking sheet. Spoon the peaches equally into the middle of each pastry square, leaving a 1-inch border on all sides. Brush the edges of the pastry with the beaten egg, fold over to make a triangle, and crimp the edges with a fork. Brush the tops with the egg and, using a sharp knife, cut small steam vents in the top of each turnover. Sprinkle with sugar. Refrigerate the pastries for 20 minutes. Transfer to the oven and bake until the pastries are puffed and golden brown, 20 to 25 minutes. Remove from the oven and transfer to wire racks to cool slightly.

To serve, cut each turnover in half and place the halves on a dessert plate. Peel, pit, and slice the remaining peach and garnish each plate with peach slices. Add a scoop of the ice cream to each plate and serve. *Makes 4 servings*

**Wine Pairing:** Late-harvest Muscat Canelli, Viognier, or Riesling

**Vanilla Ice Cream**
1 cup whole milk
1 cup heavy cream
½ cup sugar
1 vanilla bean, split lengthwise
4 large egg yolks
Pinch of salt

**Honey-Rosemary Sauce**
⅓ cup honey
2 tablespoons unsalted butter
Grated zest and juice of 1 lemon
½ teaspoon minced fresh rosemary

4 peaches, halved and pitted
1 tablespoon canola oil
Salt to taste
Fresh raspberries, rosemary sprigs, and
    edible flowers for garnish

For the ice cream: In a medium saucepan, combine the milk, cream, and sugar. Scrape the seeds from the vanilla bean into the milk mixture, then add the pods. Cook over medium heat, stirring occasionally, until bubbles appear around the edges of the pan; remove from the heat. In a small bowl, whisk the egg yolks to blend. Gradually whisk about half of the hot milk mixture into the egg yolks. Return to the pan and whisk to blend. Cook, stirring constantly, over medium heat until thick enough to coat the back of a spoon, 5 to 6 minutes; do not boil. Pour through a fine-mesh sieve into a bowl and let cool. Cover and refrigerate for at least 8 hours or up to 24 hours. Freeze in an ice-cream maker according to the manufacturer's instructions.

For the honey-rosemary sauce: In a small saucepan, combine all the ingredients. Stir over medium heat until the butter is melted. Remove from the heat and let stand for 10 minutes to blend the flavors.

For the grilled peaches: Prepare a medium fire in a charcoal grill or preheat a gas grill to medium. Oil the grill grids. Brush the peaches with the oil and sprinkle lightly with salt. Put the peaches on the grill, cut side down, and grill until marked, 2 to 3 minutes. Turn the peaches and brush the cut side with the honey-rosemary sauce. Cook, brushing 3 to 4 times with sauce, until grill-marked on second side, about 2 minutes more. Turn again, brush once more with sauce, and remove from the heat.

To serve, place 2 peach halves on each of 4 dessert plates. Top with a scoop of vanilla ice cream, drizzle with honey-rosemary sauce, and garnish with raspberries and a rosemary sprig. *Makes 4 servings*

**Wine Pairing:** Late-harvest Sonoma County Sauvignon Blanc/Semillon

109

The grape crush is in full swing, leaves turn from green to gold and orange, and chefs change their dishes from refreshing to refueling, with winter dead ahead.

The harvest of wine grapes, called "the crush," gets most of the attention in October and early November, when red varieties such as Cabernet Sauvignon, Merlot, Petite Sirah, Pinot Noir, and Zinfandel are picked and begin their journey from fruit to wine. This time of year usually brings Indian summer conditions, with days warm enough to wear shorts and evenings cool enough to call for a jacket. The air smells of fall—woodsy, like damp forest floor and fireplace smoke commingled. The last of the Gravenstein apples are baked into cakes and pies; ripe, end-of-season tomatoes are savored to the last slice, and the ones that don't mature before fall rains arrive are picked and fried, Southern style. Mushrooms play an important role in chefs' fall dishes, as do dried chiles, butternut squash, pumpkin, duck, and pork. Hot soups return, and Thanksgiving has chefs tweaking their recipes for turkey, stuffing, cranberries, and potatoes.

## WILD MUSHROOM AND GOAT CHEESE CHILE RELLENOS WITH NEW MEXICO RED CHILE SAUCE

*One of the most popular dishes on our fall menu, we make these rellenos with Anaheim chiles from our own garden. They are great as an appetizer, but they also make a good side dish for grilled hanger or skirt steak. The dried chiles for the sauce are available at Mexican markets and in the Latino section of many supermarkets.*

### GOURMET MUSHROOMS

114

*Malcolm Clark is a megastar among mycologists—those who study fungi, including mushrooms. As the founder of Gourmet Mushrooms in Sebastopol, he is credited with being the first to grow and sell commercial shiitake mushrooms in North America, beginning in 1977. Malcolm retired in 2006, yet remains as a consultant; his business partner from the start, David Law, runs the company, which currently grows six varieties of edible exotic mushrooms (trumpet royale, alba clamshell, brown clamshell, forest nameko, velvet pioppini, and nebrodini blanco) and has a seventh, maitake (also known as hen-of-the-woods) in development. They're grown organically, in sawdust reclaimed from millings rather than in manure, and the substrate left after harvesting is composted and applied to a neighboring Pinot Noir vineyard.*

*I created this dish for our vegetarian customers. It's substantial enough for a main course, yet I also like it as an accompaniment to grilled meat. Poblanos are mild, dark green triangular chiles, sometimes called pasillas in California, and no one grows them better than Lee and Wayne James of Tierra Vegetables.*

**TIERRA VEGETABLES**

*Lee James, her brother, Wayne, and his wife, Evie Truxaw, have grown chiles and other produce in Sonoma County for a quarter century. In conjunction with the Sonoma County Agricultural Preservation and Open Space District, seventeen of their twenty acres are leased from the county in an innovative partnership that supports local, small-scale agriculture. Tierra grows numerous vegetables and fruits, and sells them at its farm stand in Santa Rosa, between Highway 101 and Fulton Road, yet it's best known—and most valued by chefs—for its twenty-plus varieties of sustainably grown chiles and peppers. The Jameses' oven-roasted chipotles are a specialty, and their chipotle powder is a staple of Sonoma County cooks, both professional and amateur.*

**Red Chile Sauce**

1 teaspoon cumin seeds
5 dried New Mexico chiles
5 dried California chiles
5 ancho chiles
2 tablespoons olive oil
1 yellow onion, chopped
3 cloves garlic, sliced
2 teaspoons dried oregano, preferably
  Mexican
3 cups chicken broth
1 teaspoon kosher salt

**Chile Rellenos**

4 fresh Anaheim chiles
1 tablespoon canola or corn oil
2 tablespoons unsalted butter
1 shallot, minced
1 teaspoon minced fresh thyme
9 ounces mixed mushrooms, such as
  chanterelles, oysters, cremini, or buttons,
  sliced (3 cups)
¼ cup dry sherry
1 teaspoon kosher salt
4 ounces fresh goat cheese, such as
  Laura Chenel
1 tablespoon all-purpose flour
1 tablespoon cornstarch
2 tablespoons olive oil

Crumbled cotija cheese for sprinkling

For the chile sauce: In a dry medium skillet over medium heat, toast the cumin seeds until fragrant, 1 to 2 minutes. Grind in a spice grinder or clean coffee grinder. Stem the dried chiles and remove the seeds. Break the chiles into 1-inch pieces. Return the skillet to medium heat and toast the chiles, stirring, until fragrant, about 1 to 2 minutes. Do not allow to burn. Transfer the chiles to a bowl, add hot water to cover, and let stand for 20 minutes.

In a heavy, medium saucepan, heat the olive oil over medium heat. Add the onions and sauté until golden brown, 7 to 8 minutes. Stir in the garlic, toasted cumin, and oregano. Drain the chiles and add to the onion mixture along with the chicken broth and salt. Bring to a boil, reduce heat to a simmer, and cook for 20 minutes.

Working in batches if necessary, puree the sauce in a blender. Strain through a fine-mesh sieve. Taste and adjust the seasoning. Return to the pan and set aside.

For the rellenos: Preheat the broiler. In a medium bowl, toss the Anaheim chiles with the oil to coat and place on a baking sheet. Broil 4 to 6 inches from the heat source until the skins begin to blister, 4 to 6 minutes; turn and broil on the second side until blistered, another 4 to 6 minutes. Remove from the broiler and let cool to the touch. Peel off the skins, slit the chiles down the sides with a paring knife, and carefully remove the seeds. Set aside.

In a medium skillet, melt the butter over medium heat. Add the shallot and thyme and sauté until the shallot is translucent, about 2 minutes. Add the mushrooms and cook, stirring occasionally, until they have released most of their juices, 5 to 6 minutes. Stir in the sherry and salt and cook until the mixture is almost dry. Remove from the heat and let cool for 5 minutes. Stir in the goat cheese. Refrigerate for 10 minutes.

Mold one-fourth of the mushroom mixture into an oval and stuff it into a chile; repeat with the remaining filling and chiles. If the chiles tend to fall open, secure each with a toothpick. In a shallow bowl, combine the flour and cornstarch; stir with a whisk to blend. Dredge the chiles in the flour mixture to coat.

Reheat the chile sauce over low heat. Meanwhile, in a medium nonstick skillet, heat the olive oil over medium heat. Add the chiles and fry until browned and crisp, 2 to 3 minutes on each side. Remove the toothpicks. Ladle the hot chile sauce onto each of 4 salad plates and top each with a fried stuffed chile. Garnish with the cotija cheese. *Makes 4 first-course servings or side dishes*

**Wine Pairing:** Dry Creek Valley Zinfandel or Syrah

116

**Cilantro Cream**
2 cups heavy cream
⅓ cup chopped fresh cilantro
1 teaspoon grated lime zest
2 tablespoons fresh lime juice
Salt and freshly ground pepper to taste

8 poblano chiles

**Basmati-Butternut Stuffing**
1½ cups water
1 cup basmati rice
¼ cup pine nuts
2 cups ½-inch-diced butternut squash
1 teaspoon canola oil
¼ cup dried currants
¼ cup chopped fresh cilantro
½ cup fresh goat cheese, such as
    Laura Chenel, at room temperature
Salt and freshly ground pepper to taste

For the cilantro cream: In a saucepan, bring the cream to a boil over high heat. Reduce the heat to low and simmer until reduced by half, 30 to 40 minutes. Stir in the cilantro, lime zest, and lime juice. Season with salt and pepper.

Preheat the broiler. Place the poblano chiles on a baking sheet and broil until blistered, 4 to 6 minutes on each side. Place in a plastic bag, let stand until cool enough to handle, and peel. Cut a slit in the side of each chile, carefully remove the seeds and membranes, and set aside.

For the stuffing: Preheat the oven to 450°F. In a medium saucepan, bring the water to a boil. Add the basmati rice, reduce the heat to low, cover, and cook until rice is tender, about 17 minutes. Remove from the heat and fluff with a fork. Spread the rice on a baking sheet and let cool for 5 minutes. In a small, dry skillet, stir the pine nuts over medium heat until lightly toasted and fragrant, about 5 minutes. Remove from the heat and set aside. In a roasting pan, toss the butternut squash with the oil. Roast until tender, about 10 to 15 minutes. Remove from the oven and let cool.

In a large bowl, combine the rice, pine nuts, currants, cooled butternut squash, and cilantro. Stir in the cheese until very thoroughly combined. Season with salt and pepper.

Preheat the oven to 400°F. Gently stuff the chiles with the rice mixture (depending on the size of the chiles, you may have a little left over). Secure the slits with toothpicks, if desired. Place the chiles in a shallow baking dish and add ¼ inch water. Cover the dish with aluminum foil. Bake until heated through, 12 to 15 minutes. Remove the toothpicks and place the stuffed chiles on plates in a pool of the cilantro cream. *Makes 8 first-course servings or 4 main-dish servings*

**Wine Pairing:** Dry Creek Valley or Russian River Valley Sauvignon Blanc

117

## BUTTERNUT SQUASH AND APPLE SOUP
## WITH LEMON CREAM AND CRISPY SAGE

*Fall is all about apples and winter squash. Fresh apples and cider vinegar—*
*like Nana Mae's Organics Sonoma County vinegar—give sweetness and acidity to*
*this traditional soup. Look for your own locally grown apples.*

*Butternut squash has a comforting, mellow flavor and is a foundation of fall cooking. The sweetness of the apple and the smokiness of the bacon give this soup a depth of flavor that warms the soul during fall. It also freezes well.*

# BUTTERNUT SQUASH AND APPLE SOUP WITH

## LEMON CREAM AND CRISPY SAGE

½ cup (1 stick) unsalted butter
1 butternut squash (about 2 pounds), peeled,
     seeded, and cubed
1 yellow onion, chopped
2 green apples (about 1 pound total), peeled,
     cored, and chopped
6 fresh sage leaves
4 cups chicken stock or broth
2 teaspoons organic apple cider vinegar,
     preferably Nana Mae's
1 tablespoon kosher salt
½ cup heavy cream

**Lemon Cream**
½ cup crème fraîche
½ teaspoon grated lemon zest
1½ tablespoons fresh lemon juice
Salt and freshly ground pepper to taste

**Crispy Sage Leaves**
2 tablespoons unsalted butter
10 fresh sage leaves
Salt for sprinkling

For the soup: In a large soup pot, melt the
butter over medium-high heat until lightly
browned. Stir in the squash, onion, apples,
and the 6 sage leaves. Cook, stirring often,
until the vegetables and apples are golden
brown, about 10 minutes.

Stir in the stock, vinegar, and salt and bring
to a boil. Reduce the heat to a simmer and
cook until the squash is tender when
pierced, about 15 minutes. Stir in the cream.
Working in batches, puree the soup in a
blender until smooth. Return to the soup pot
and keep warm.

For the lemon cream: In a small bowl,
combine all the ingredients and stir until
blended.

For the crispy sage leaves: In a small
saucepan, melt the butter over medium heat
until it foams. Add the 10 sage leaves and
sauté until crisp, 45 seconds to 1 minute.
Using a slotted spoon, transfer to paper
towels to drain. Sprinkle lightly with salt,
and break the leaves into smaller pieces.

Ladle the hot soup into shallow bowls. Top
each with a dollop of lemon cream and a
sprinkling of sage leaves and serve at once.
*Makes 6 to 8 first-course servings*

**Wine Pairing:** Sonoma County Pinot Gris,
Riesling, or blanc de blancs sparkling wine

1 butternut squash (about 2½ pounds),
  halved lengthwise and seeded
1 tablespoon olive oil
Salt and freshly ground pepper to taste
2 tablespoons unsalted butter
1 slice apple wood–smoked bacon, coarsely
  chopped
1 yellow onion, sliced
3 to 4 peeled cloves garlic
2 Granny Smith apples, peeled, cored, and
  diced
6 cups chicken broth or stock
1 cup apple cider or juice
½ cup heavy cream
½ cup crème fraîche for drizzling

**Smoked Paprika Oil**
1 teaspoon Spanish Smoked sweet paprika
½ cup vegetable oil

Preheat the oven to 375°F. Brush the cut sides of the squash with the olive oil. Sprinkle with salt and pepper, place cut side down on a baking sheet, and roast until soft, about 45 minutes. Remove from the oven and let cool, then scoop the flesh into a bowl.

In a large soup pot, melt the butter over medium-high heat. Add the bacon and cook until fragrant, 2 to 3 minutes. Add the onion, garlic, and apples. Sauté until the onion is translucent, 3 to 4 minutes. Add the squash, chicken broth, and apple juice. Bring to a boil, reduce the heat to a simmer, and cook until apples are very tender, 30 minutes.

For the paprika oil: Heat the paprika and vegetable oil in a small pan over medium heat for 2 minutes, stirring until the paprika is blended into the oil. Remove from the heat and let cool for 15 minutes. Strain through a fine-mesh sieve into a small pitcher and set aside.

Working in batches, puree the soup in a blender until smooth. Add the cream and season with salt and pepper to taste.

Ladle into warmed soup bowls and garnish with crème fraîche and a drizzle of the paprika oil. *Makes 8 first-course servings*

**Wine Pairing:** Sonoma County off-dry Gewürztraminer

121

## APPLE WOOD–SMOKED PORK CHOPS WITH FRESH APPLESAUCE, BRAISED RAINBOW CHARD, AND CORN BREAD STUFFING

*This is our signature dish, which has been on the menu since we opened. A modern take on the American classic, pork chops and applesauce, it's a little Southern, a little sweet, a little sour, and a little savory.*

*Most pork is raised to be very lean these days; we purchase heritage pork because it has more intramuscular fat, and fat means flavor. The key to cooking juicy pork chops is to brine them first.*

## PORK CHOPS WITH FENNEL-APPLE SALAD AND POTATO PANCAKES

## APPLE WOOD–SMOKED PORK CHOPS WITH FRESH APPLESAUCE, BRAISED RAINBOW CHARD, AND CORN BREAD STUFFING

**Pork Chops**

One 12-ounce bottle microbrewed beer
¼ cup kosher salt
¼ cup packed brown sugar
1 tablespoon molasses
1 tablespoon Sriracha hot sauce
4 cloves garlic, thinly sliced
2 teaspoons black peppercorns
2 teaspoons minced fresh thyme
2 cups water
4 thick-cut bone-in pork chops
    (about 2½ pounds total)

**Applesauce**

1 cup granulated sugar
4 Granny Smith apples (about 2 pounds total),
    peeled, cored, and cut into ½-inch dice
2 tablespoons fresh lime juice
Pinch of kosher salt
½ teaspoon ground cinnamon

3 cups apple wood smoking chips

**Corn Bread Stuffing**

2 tablespoons olive oil
1 andouille sausage (about 8 ounces), diced
1 yellow onion, diced
1 stalk celery, diced
1 green bell pepper, seeded, deribbed, and
    diced
¼ cup chopped fresh flat-leaf parsley
2 tablespoons chopped fresh sage leaves
½ cup chicken broth or stock
4 cups crumbled corn bread (about half an
    8-inch square pan of corn bread)
Salt and freshly ground pepper to taste

**Rainbow Chard**

2 bunches rainbow chard or Swiss chard
    (about 1½ pounds total), stemmed
2 tablespoons olive oil
1 small red onion, thinly sliced
1 tablespoon organic apple cider vinegar,
    such as Nana Mae's
½ cup chicken broth
Salt and freshly ground pepper to taste

For the pork chops: In a large bowl, combine the beer, salt, sugar, molasses, Sriracha hot sauce, garlic, peppercorns, and thyme. Add the water and stir until the salt and sugar have dissolved. Add the pork chops, cover, and refrigerate for 12 hours.

For the applesauce: In a large, heavy skillet, melt the sugar over medium-high heat, shaking the pan frequently, until it just begins to turn golden, 3 to 4 minutes. Add the apples, lime juice, and salt. (The caramel will clump, but will melt as the applesauce cooks; add a little water to melt it if necessary.) Cook, stirring often and adjusting the heat as needed to prevent scorching, until the apples are soft and caramelized a light brown color, about 15 minutes. Remove from the heat and stir in the cinnamon. Set aside.

For the corn bread stuffing: Preheat the oven to 350°F. In a large skillet, heat the oil over medium-high heat. Add the sausage and cook, turning, until well browned on all sides, 5 to 6 minutes. Add the onion, celery, and green pepper and sauté until the onion is

translucent and soft, 6 to 8 minutes. Stir in the parsley, sage, and chicken broth and bring to a boil. Put the corn bread in a large, shallow 8-cup baking dish and pour the onion mixture over the corn bread. Stir gently to coat and season with salt and pepper. Transfer to the oven and bake until browned, about 20 minutes. Remove from the oven and keep warm.

While the stuffing is baking, prepare a charcoal grill for indirect-heat cooking, mounding the hot coals on one side of the grill. Remove the pork from the brine (discard the brine) and pat dry. Soak the apple wood chips in warm water for 10 minutes; drain. Sprinkle the apple wood chips over the coals and place the pork chops on the indirect-heat area of the grill (not over the coals). Cover the grill and smoke the pork chops for 20 minutes. Remove the cover and open the vents to increase the heat; if needed, add a few more coals. Move the pork chops to the direct-heat area of the grill and cook for 2 to 3 minutes on each side for medium. Transfer to a plate and tent with aluminum foil; let rest for 5 minutes.

For the rainbow chard: Coarsely chop the chard leaves. In a large skillet, heat the oil over high heat. Add the onion and sauté until golden, about 5 minutes. Working in batches, add the chard and cook until wilted, 2 to 3 minutes. Add the vinegar and chicken broth, reduce the heat to medium, and cook until the chard is tender, about 5 minutes.

Season with salt and pepper. Set aside and keep warm.

To serve, reheat the applesauce over low heat. Spoon a mound of corn bread stuffing into the center of each of 4 dinner plates. Top each with one-fourth of the chard. Lean a pork chop against each mound and add a spoonful of applesauce. *Makes 4 main-course servings*

**Wine Pairing:** Sonoma County Riesling or Syrah

### Brined Pork Chops

4 cups water
3 tablespoons kosher salt
2 tablespoons cider vinegar
1 tablespoon packed brown sugar
1 tablespoon coriander seeds
1 tablespoon fennel seeds
2 bay leaves
4 thick pork chops (about 10 ounces each)

### Fennel-Apple Salad

1 apple, peeled and cored
1 bulb fennel (12 ounces), trimmed
1½ teaspoons cider vinegar
½ teaspoon sugar
½ teaspoon grated lemon zest
1 tablespoon extra-virgin olive oil
Salt and freshly ground pepper to taste

### Fennel Pollen Aioli

1 garlic clove
¼ teaspoon kosher salt
1 large egg yolk at room temperature
2 teaspoons fresh lemon juice
½ teaspoon Dijon mustard
¼ cup extra-virgin olive oil
3 tablespoons canola oil
Big pinch of fennel pollen

### Potato Pancakes

2 large Yukon Gold potatoes, peeled
½ yellow onion
1 large egg, beaten
2 tablespoons all-purpose flour
Salt and freshly ground pepper to taste
About 2 cups canola oil for frying

For the pork chops: In a medium saucepan, combine the water, salt, vinegar, sugar, coriander seeds, fennel seeds, and bay leaves. Bring to a boil over high heat, then remove from the heat, and let cool completely. Pour over the pork chops in a bowl, cover, and refrigerate for 6 to 8 hours.

Meanwhile, for the fennel-apple salad: Using a mandoline or very sharp knife, cut the apple and fennel into paper thin slices. Put the slices in a bowl, cover with ice water, and soak for 30 minutes. In a small bowl, whisk the vinegar, sugar, lemon zest, and olive oil together. Season with salt and pepper. Drain the fennel and apple well and toss with the vinaigrette.

For the aioli: On a cutting board, mince the garlic with the salt and mash with the flat edge of the knife until it forms a paste. In a bowl, whisk the egg yolk, lemon juice, and mustard together. Whisk in the garlic paste. Combine the oils in a measuring cup and, whisking constantly, add them to the yolk mixture a few drops at a time until the mixture is emulsified and all the oil is incorporated. (If the mixture separates, stop adding the oil and continue whisking until mixture comes together, then resume adding oil.) Whisk in the fennel pollen and season with salt and pepper. If the aioli is too thick, whisk in 1 or 2 drops of water. Cover and refrigerate until ready to use.

For the potato pancakes: Using the large holes on a box grater, shred the potato and onion into a bowl of hot water. Drain, cover with more hot water, and drain again. Cover with cold water, rinse, then drain very well. Spread the shreds on a clean kitchen towel, roll it up, and wring to squeeze out as much water as you can. Empty the shreds into a bowl and add the egg, flour, salt, and pepper; stir to combine thoroughly. Gently shape the mixture into 4 equal cakes.

In a large, heavy skillet, heat ½ inch oil over high heat to 375°F (a shred of potato will sizzle and brown almost instantly), and add the potato pancakes. Flatten each gently with a metal spatula and fry until golden brown on the bottom, 2 to 3 minutes. Flip over and cook until golden brown on second side and tender throughout, 3 to 4 minutes more.

Prepare a medium-hot fire in a charcoal grill, or preheat a gas grill to medium-high. Drain the pork chops and pat dry. Grill for 6 or 7 minutes on each side for medium. Place a potato pancake on each of 4 dinner plates and top each with a pork chop. Add a spoonful of aioli and the fennel-apple salad. Garnish with fennel fronds if desired and serve. *Makes 4 main-course servings*

**Wine Pairing:** Sonoma County Riesling or Chardonnay

125

## NEW ORLEANS RED BEAN "CASSOULET" WITH CRISPY DUCK, HAM HOCK, AND ANDOUILLE SAUSAGE

*My wife, Susan, and I love traveling in the South, especially in and around New Orleans. I am always searching out the best red beans and rice I can find there. This version of cassoulet uses our favorite Southern ingredients. It's even better the next day.*

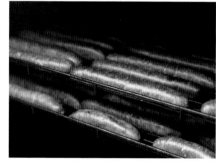

## DECONSTRUCTED CASSOULET

*We love the beauty of cassoulet. All the components can be prepared 3 or 4 days ahead and in stages. The duck confit, if covered with the duck fat, will last 2 to 3 weeks. The pork belly will keep for 1 week after cooking. The beans will keep 2 to 3 days. Once you have the components prepared you can put this dinner together in under an hour. The breast from the duck can be used in the duck breast recipe on page 69. Be sure to buy good pork and garlic sausage. You will have leftover pork belly, which you can wrap and freeze. It is delicious served as a starter with a little sweet sauce. I think of it as "the new foie gras." I have "deconstructed" this dish because after 3 or 4 bites I find myself wanting individual bites of different flavors.*

127

## NEW ORLEANS RED BEAN "CASSOULET" WITH

## CRISPY DUCK, HAM HOCK, AND ANDOUILLE SAUSAGE

6 duck confit legs in duck fat,
store bought and already prepared
6 cups chicken stock or broth
1 ham hock
1 pound dried light red kidney beans,
rinsed and picked over
3 thick slices bacon, diced
1 andouille sausage (8 ounces), diced
1 red bell pepper, seeded, deribbed, and
diced
1 green bell pepper, seeded, deribbed,
and diced
4 green onions, sliced
3 cloves garlic, thinly sliced
½ cup plus 3 tablespoons chopped fresh
flat-leaf parsley
2 teaspoons minced fresh thyme
¼ teaspoon cayenne pepper
¼ teaspoon red pepper flakes
1 bay leaf
4 cups water
Salt and freshly ground pepper to taste
1¼ cups fresh bread crumbs
½ cup grated Parmesan cheese
2 tablespoons olive oil
1 tablespoon Zin Dry Rub (recipe follows)

Remove the duck confit legs from the fat; reserve ¼ cup of the fat and set the legs aside.

In a large soup pot, bring the chicken stock to a simmer over medium heat. Add the ham hock and cook until tender, 1 hour.

Add the beans, reserved duck fat, bacon, sausage, red and green peppers, green onions, garlic, the ½ cup parsley, the thyme, cayenne, pepper flakes, bay leaf, and water to the soup pot. Increase the heat to high and bring to a full rolling boil; cook for 10 minutes. Reduce the heat to a simmer and cook until the beans are tender, about 2 hours, adding water as needed to prevent them from becoming too dry. Using tongs, transfer the ham hock to a plate and let cool to the touch. Remove and discard the skin. Shred the meat and stir it into the beans. Season with salt and pepper and let cool. Cover and refrigerate for at least 8 hours or up to 24 hours.

Preheat the oven to 350°F. In a food processor, combine the bread crumbs, Parmesan, the 3 tablespoons parsley, and the olive oil. Pulse to mix evenly. Divide the red beans among six 1½-cup ramekins or ovenproof soup bowls and top evenly with the bread crumb mixture.

Put the duck legs in a baking dish and sprinkle evenly with the dry rub. Place the ramekins of beans and the dish of duck in oven and bake until the beans are golden brown and bubbling and the duck legs are crisp and golden, about 25 minutes. Place a duck leg on top of each casserole and serve. *Makes 6 main-course servings*

**Wine Pairing:** Sonoma County Zinfandel or medium-bodied Merlot

**Zin Dry Rub**
3 tablespoons sweet Hungarian paprika
3 tablespoons kosher salt
3 tablespoons garlic powder
1½ tablespoons dried oregano
1½ tablespoons dried thyme
1½ tablespoons sugar
4 teaspoons freshly ground black pepper
4 teaspoons onion powder
1½ teaspoons cayenne pepper
1½ teaspoons ancho chile powder

In a small bowl, combine all the ingredients and stir to blend well. Store in an airtight container for up to 2 weeks. *Makes 1 heaping cup*

### Duck Confit and Stock

1 duck (5 or 6 pounds)
2 duck legs (including thighs), about 1 pound total
2 tablespoons kosher salt
3 bay leaves
3 sprigs thyme
Approximately 1 cup of duck fat, melted, if needed
2 carrots, peeled and cut into chunks
1 yellow onion, cut into chunks
3 stalks celery, cut into chunks
8 black peppercorns

### Pork Belly

1 pound pork belly
1 teaspoon kosher salt
1 teaspoon canola oil
1 yellow onion, sliced
4 peeled cloves garlic
¾ cup apple cider or juice
2 cups duck stock (above)

### White Beans

2 cups dried white beans, such as cannellini beans
2 tablespoons duck fat
3 cloves garlic, minced
1 cup diced yellow onion
1 cup diced fennel
6 cups duck stock (above)
Salt and freshly ground pepper to taste

### Bread Crumb Topping

1½ cups panko (Japanese bread crumbs)
2 teaspoons minced garlic
2 tablespoons chopped fresh flat-leaf parsley
2 tablespoons duck fat, melted

### Sautéed Spinach

3 tablespoons unsalted butter
3 shallots, thinly sliced
1 pound of spinach (about 2 bunches), stemmed and rinsed

Salt and freshly ground pepper to taste
4 fresh garlic-pork sausages
½ teaspoon canola oil
Caperberries for garnish

For the duck confit: Cut the legs of the whole duck, including the thighs, off at the joint; trim and reserve the excess fat. Trim and reserve the excess fat from the other 2 duck legs. Sprinkle all 4 duck legs with the kosher salt and put them in a bowl. Crumble 2 of the bay leaves and sprinkle them with the thyme sprigs over the duck legs. Cover with plastic wrap, set a second bowl on top, and add heavy weights (such as canned goods or a brick). Refrigerate for 12 hours. Rinse the legs and pat dry.

Meanwhile, with a sharp boning knife, remove the duck breasts, trim and reserve the excess fat, and reserve the breasts for another use. Cut the rest of the fat and fatty skin from the carcass and reserve. Reserve the carcass. Put all the reserved fat and skin in a food processor and process until smooth and creamy. Put the mixture in a heavy saucepan and cook over low heat until the fat is a clear yellow and the solids are well browned, 45 minutes to 1 hour. Strain through a fine-mesh sieve lined with cheese-cloth and let cool (reserve the cracklings for other uses). You should have about 1½ cups duck fat. Use now, or cover and refrigerate for up to 1 week or in the freezer for up to 6 months; melt in a saucepan over low heat before using.

Preheat the oven to 250°F. Place the duck legs in a deep, 2-quart baking dish and cover with the melted duck fat. If the fat does not cover the duck legs, add more to cover. Bake until the legs are very tender and skin is golden, 4 hours. Remove from the oven and let cool. Making sure the duck legs are completely immersed in fat, cover and refrigerate for at least 1 day or up to 3 weeks.

129

*(recipe continues next page)*

For the duck stock: Preheat the oven to 375°F. Place the reserved duck carcass in a roasting pan and roast until browned, 40 to 45 minutes. Transfer to a stockpot and add cold water to cover. Bring to a boil over high heat, reduce the heat to a simmer, and skim off the foam. Add the carrots, onion, celery, the remaining bay leaf, and the peppercorns. Simmer for 3 hours, skimming the foam as needed. Strain and let cool. Cover, and refrigerate for up to 3 days. You should have about 8 cups of stock.

For the pork belly: Sprinkle the belly with the salt and place on a plate. Cover with plastic wrap and top with a plate to weigh it down. Refrigerate for 12 hours.

Preheat the oven to 275°F. In a large oven-proof skillet, heat the oil over high heat. Add the pork belly, fattiest side down, and cook until golden on the bottom, 4 to 5 minutes. Transfer to a plate and add the onion and garlic to the pan. Place the pork belly on top of the onion and garlic, seared side up, and add the apple juice and duck stock. Cover with aluminum foil and bake until pork belly is soft and easily pierced with a small knife, about 2½ hours. Remove from the oven and let cool. Transfer the pork belly to a plate (discard the onion and liquid), cover, and refrigerate overnight.

For the beans: Rinse and pick over the beans. Soak the beans in cold water to cover by 2 inches for 12 hours. In a soup pot, melt the duck fat over medium-high heat. Add the garlic, onion, and fennel and sauté until the onion is tender, about 8 minutes. Drain the beans and add the beans and stock to the pot. Bring to a boil, reduce the heat to a simmer, and cook until the beans are tender, 1 to 2 hours. Season with salt and pepper and let cool. Use now, or cover and refrigerate for up to 3 days.

For the bread crumb topping: In a small bowl, combine all the ingredients and stir to blend.

For the sautéed spinach: In a large skillet, melt the butter over medium-high heat and cook until browned, 2 to 3 minutes. Add the shallots and cook, stirring, until golden, about 2 minutes. Add the spinach until the pan is full and cover until the spinach is wilted, 2 to 3 minutes; repeat, adding remaining spinach in batches. Season with salt and pepper and place in a colander to drain any excess liquid. Set aside and keep warm.

Preheat the oven to 375°F. Divide the beans among four 6-cup ramekins. Top equally with the bread-crumb topping and bake until golden brown, 35 minutes. Meanwhile, remove the duck legs from the fat and place in a baking pan. Prick the sausages with a sharp knife and place in a baking pan. Bake until the duck is golden brown and the sausages are cooked through, 20 to 25 minutes. Remove from the oven and keep warm.

Meanwhile, cut four ¾-inch-thick slices from the pork belly and reserve the rest for another use in the freezer, wrapped well in plastic wrap. In a small ovenproof skillet, heat the oil over high heat. Add the pork belly slices and cook until golden on the bottom, 1 minute. Transfer to the oven and cook until the pork belly is crisp on the bottom and soft on top, 4 minutes. Remove from the oven, turn the pork belly over, and sear in the hot pan for 30 seconds.

To serve, place a ramekin on each of 4 dinner plates. Top each with a piece of pork belly, browned side up, and garnish the plate with caperberries. Spoon a mound of sautéed spinach onto each plate, top with a duck leg and a sausage, and serve. *Makes 4 main-course servings*

**Wine Pairing:** Russian River Valley Pinot Noir or Sonoma Coast Syrah

131

# APPLE "UPSIDE-DOWN" CAKE WITH
# SALTY CARAMEL AND WHIPPED CREAM

*This spiced version of pineapple upside-down cake is made with apples and has a caramel topping with contrasting flavors of sweet and salty.*

## GRAVENSTEIN APPLES

*Before western Sonoma County was wine country, it was apple country, and the Gravenstein ruled the kingdom. But as wine production boomed, and grapes commanded higher prices than apples, many orchards were replanted to vineyards; where Gravensteins once grew, Pinot Noir now thrives. Still, a handful of dedicated folks continue to grown Gravensteins, which are known for their versatility for use in applesauce, cider, pies, cakes, and of course, being eaten out of hand. It's a crisp, sweet-tart apple that ripens in early August and has a very short, 2-month season. Famous horticulturist Luther Burbank, based in Santa Rosa, praised the variety, saying, "It has often been said that if the Gravenstein could be had throughout the year, no other apple need be grown." The Gravenstein Apple Fair, held every August in Sebastopol, celebrates this agricultural treasure.*

## BUTTERY GRAVENSTEIN APPLE CAKE
## WITH MASCARPONE SHERBET

This dessert celebrates the sweet and tart flavors of the Gravenstein apple. The warm, dry days and cool nights of Sonoma County make for ideal growing conditions for Gravensteins. First planted in 1811, they were treasured for their versatility and full-bodied flavor. The twisted trunks of these magnificent trees can support a thirty-foot canopy of beautiful, aromatic blossoms in springtime. In North America, they are the first apples ready for the market. Here in Sebastopol, they are honored every year by the Spring Apple Blossom Festival and again at the Gravenstein Harvest Festival. If Gravenstein apples are not available, ripe Granny Smith apples may be substituted.

133

**Salty Caramel**

1 cup heavy cream
5 tablespoons unsalted butter
2 teaspoons fleur de sel (a French
   sea salt)
1½ cups sugar
¼ cup light corn syrup
¼ cup water

**Apple Spice Cake**

1½ cups all-purpose flour
1½ teaspoons baking powder
¾ teaspoon kosher salt
1 teaspoon ground ginger
½ teaspoon ground cinnamon
½ cup (1 stick) unsalted butter at room
   temperature
⅔ cup sugar
1 teaspoon vanilla extract
2 large eggs
½ cup sour cream
4 Granny Smith apples (about 1½ pounds
   total), peeled, cored, and cut into
   ½-inch dice

Lightly sweetened whipped cream for
   serving

For the caramel: In a small saucepan, combine the cream, butter, and fleur de sel. Set over medium-high heat and bring to a boil. Remove from the heat and set aside.

In a medium, heavy pan, whisk together the sugar, corn syrup, and water. Cook over high heat, without stirring, until the sugar is dissolved and turns a deep golden brown, 10 to 12 minutes. Remove from the heat and carefully add the cream mixture (it will foam). Stir until smooth and set aside.

For the apple cake: Preheat the oven to 350°F and butter a 9-inch round cake pan.

In a medium bowl, combine the flour, baking powder, salt, ginger, and cinnamon. Stir with a whisk to blend. Using an electric mixer on medium speed, cream the butter and sugar until light and fluffy. Beat in the vanilla, then beat in the eggs, one at a time, beating well after each addition. Beat in the sour cream and the flour mixture at low speed, alternately stopping to scrape down the sides of the bowl once or twice. Fold 1 cup of the diced apple into the batter.

Pour three-fourths of the caramel into the prepared pan. Top evenly with the remaining apples. Scrape in the cake batter and smooth the top. Place in the oven and bake until a toothpick inserted into the center of the cake comes out clean, 50 to 60 minutes. Remove from the oven and let cool on a wire rack for 10 minutes.

Run a knife around the edge of cake. Invert a large plate over the top of the cake and carefully flip the cake over to unmold. Remove the pan and replace any apples that are stuck to the pan. Let cool until warm or room temperature.

Cut the cake into 8 wedges and place on dessert plates. If the remaining caramel has thickened too much to pour, warm it briefly in the microwave or on the stove top until pourable. Drizzle each cake wedge with caramel, top with a dollop of whipped cream, and serve. *Makes 8 servings*

**Wine Pairing:** Sonoma County late-harvest Riesling

134

**Mascarpone Sherbet**
½ cup granulated sugar
½ cup water
1 cup (8 ounces) mascarpone cheese
    at room temperature
¾ cup light corn syrup
1 cup buttermilk
1 cup whole milk
1 teaspoon vanilla extract
2 teaspoons fresh lemon juice
¼ teaspoon kosher salt

**Gravenstein Apple Cake**
¾ cup plus 1 tablespoon unsalted butter
3 Gravenstein apples, peeled, cored, and
    cut into ¼-inch-thick slices
¾ cup all-purpose flour
¼ teaspoon baking powder
¼ teaspoon salt
2 large eggs
1 large egg yolk
1 cup granulated sugar
1 teaspoon vanilla extract
¼ teaspoon each grated lemon and
    orange zest
Confectioners' sugar for dusting

For the sherbet: In a small saucepan, combine the sugar and water. Bring to a boil over medium heat, stirring until the sugar is dissolved. Remove from the heat and let cool completely. You should have about ½ cup simple syrup.

Using an electric mixer on high speed, beat the mascarpone with the corn syrup until soft peaks form. Add the simple syrup, buttermilk, milk, vanilla, lemon juice, and salt and beat until thoroughly combined. Freeze in an ice-cream maker according to the manufacturer's instructions. The sherbet will be softly frozen; if desired, spoon into a container, cover airtight, and freeze until firm, at least 3 hours, before serving.

For the apple cake: Preheat the oven to 375°F. Generously butter a 9-inch round cake pan, line the bottom with a round of parchment paper, and butter the paper.

In a large skillet, melt the butter over low heat. Pour 6 tablespoons of the butter into a small bowl and reserve. Add the apple slices to the butter in the skillet, increase the heat to medium, and cook, stirring occasionally, until the apples are tender, about 10 minutes. Remove from the heat and set aside.

In a small bowl, combine the flour, baking powder, and salt. Stir with a whisk to blend. In a large bowl, beat the eggs and egg yolk until blended. Add the reserved melted butter, the sugar, vanilla, and lemon and orange zest to the egg mixture and stir to combine. Stir in the flour mixture and the apples.

Spoon the batter into the prepared pan, smoothing the top. Bake until the cake is browned, 30 to 35 minutes, or until a toothpick inserted into the center of the cake comes out clean. Transfer to a wire rack and let cool in the pan for 5 minutes.

Invert the cake onto a plate and lift off the pan. Peel off the parchment paper, then invert the cake again onto the rack and let cool completely. Just before serving, dust the top of the cake with confectioners' sugar. To serve, cut into wedges and top each with a scoop of the mascarpone sherbet. *Makes 8 to 10 servings*

**Wine Pairing:** Late-harvest Sauvignon Blanc or late-harvest Chardonnay

135

## SOUTHERN BREAD PUDDING WITH BOURBON SAUCE

*Bread pudding is one of our most popular desserts at Zin. We do several different variations, such as chocolate and dried cherry, and maple pecan. Bread pudding is traditional all across the American South, but most people associate it with New Orleans. It's is a great way to use up stale bread and that bottle of bourbon that has been gathering dust in your liquor cabinet. This is still my favorite version.*

*This is, hands down, the most popular dessert at Syrah. My inspiration came from my father, who is a chef, a brutally honest critic, and a huge fan of bread pudding. We ordered the dish everywhere we went, and after many trials, I came up with this recipe. I've kept it secret until now. The quality of the bread—I use Della Fattoria from Petaluma—is crucial to the success of the dish.*

### DELLA FATTORIA BREAD

137

*Della Fattoria has spoiled Sonoma County bread-lovers since 1995, when Kathleen Weber began baking her hand-shaped loaves in Petaluma. Inspired by chef Alice Waters and Carol Field, author of "The Italian Baker," Kathleen refined her ingredients (Della Fattoria's own starter, organic flour, and Brittany sea salt) and techniques (baking in wood-fired brick ovens) until her hobby became an artisanal business, with Northern California restaurants clamoring for her Campagne country French loaf and breads studded with olives, pumpkin seeds, walnuts, and currants. The sea salt–encrusted Meyer lemon–rosemary round is a stunningly complex bread and a favorite of Syrah customers. Kathleen's husband, Ed, fires the ovens; their son, Aaron, and daughter, Elisa, play prominent roles in the business.*

**Bread Pudding**
8 ounces sourdough bread, crusts
    removed, cut into ¾-inch cubes
1 cup heavy cream
½ cup raisins
6 tablespoons bourbon
2 large eggs
½ cup granulated sugar
1 tablespoon vanilla extract

**Bourbon Sauce**
½ cup (1 stick) unsalted butter
6 tablespoons bourbon
1 cup granulated sugar
1 large egg

Confectioners' sugar for dusting

For the bread puddings: Preheat the oven to 350°F. Spray four 1-cup ramekins with nonstick cooking spray. Set them on a baking sheet.

In a large shallow bowl, combine the bread cubes and cream. Mash them together gently and let soak for 30 minutes. In a small bowl, combine the raisins and bourbon; let soak for 20 minutes, then drain.

In a medium bowl, whisk the eggs and sugar together until pale and thick. Add the vanilla and soaked raisins, then gently stir into the bread mixture. Spoon equally into the ramekins and use a toothpick to poke any visible raisins back into the center of the puddings.

Bake until golden brown, 30 to 40 minutes. Let cool slightly, then unmold onto 4 dessert plates.

For the bourbon sauce: In a small saucepan, melt the butter over low heat with the bourbon and sugar. Cook, stirring occasionally, for 10 minutes.

In a small bowl, whisk the egg to combine. Gradually whisk in the warm butter mixture and return to the pan. Cook over medium heat, whisking constantly, until the sauce coats the back of a spoon, 3 to 5 minutes. Pour through a fine-mesh sieve into a bowl.

To serve, dust the warm bread puddings with confectioners' sugar and drizzle with the warm bourbon sauce. Pass additional sauce at the table. *Makes 4 servings*

**Wine Pairing:** Late-harvest Riesling or tawny port–style dessert wine

**Bread Pudding**
2 teaspoons ground cinnamon
8 ounces French bread, cut into 1-inch
   cubes (about 8 cups)
3 large eggs
4 large egg yolks
¾ cup sugar
1¼ cups heavy cream
1¼ cups whole milk
Pinch of salt
¼ cup whiskey
1½ teaspoons vanilla extract
¾ cup dried currants

**Caramel Sauce**
1 cup sugar
1 tablespoon light corn syrup
Pinch of salt
2 tablespoons water
1 cup heavy cream

For the bread puddings: Preheat the oven to 375°F. Butter a shallow 8-cup baking dish and sprinkle with sugar. In a large bowl, sprinkle the cinnamon over the bread cubes and toss to combine.

In a medium heatproof bowl, whisk the eggs, egg yolks, and sugar together until pale and thick. Whisk in the cream, milk, salt, whiskey, and vanilla. Place the bowl over a saucepan of barely simmering water (but not touching the water) and stir until very warm, 6 to 8 minutes. Pour over the bread cubes, stir in the currants, and let stand for 20 minutes.

Pour into the prepared baking dish and set it in a roasting pan. Pour hot water into the roasting pan to come halfway up the sides of the baking dish. Cover with aluminum foil and bake until almost set, 30 minutes. Uncover and bake until set and lightly browned, about 20 minutes longer. Let cool.

For the caramel sauce, in a saucepan, combine the sugar, corn syrup, salt, and water. Stir over medium heat until the sugar is dissolved. Increase the heat to high and boil without stirring, swirling the pan occasionally, until the syrup is a deep golden amber color, 4 to 6 minutes. Reduce the heat to low and very carefully stir in the cream in a slow, steady stream (the sauce will bubble and foam). Cook, stirring, until smooth, 2 to 3 minutes.

To serve, cut the warm bread pudding into 8 equal servings and transfer to dessert plates. Drizzle with the warm caramel sauce and pass more sauce at the table. Garnish with whipped cream, if desired. *Makes 8 servings*

**Wine Pairing:** Late-harvest Riesling or Sauvignon Blanc

139

# resources

## restaurants

**Syrah Bistro**
205 Fifth Street
Santa Rosa, CA 95401
707-568-4002
www.syrahbistro.com

**Jackson's Bar & Oven**
135 Fourth Street
Santa Rosa, CA 95401
707-545-6900
www.jacksonsbarandoven.com

**Zin Restaurant & Wine Bar**
344 Center Street
Healdsburg, CA 95448
707-473-0946
www.zinrestaurant.com

## purveyors

**Bellwether Farms**
9999 Valley Ford Road
Petaluma, CA 94952
888-527-8606
www.bellwethercheese.com
*Artisanal fresh and aged sheep's milk and cow's milk cheeses, sold by mail order and nationally at fine cheese shops and grocers, including Whole Foods. No retail sales at this location.*

**Clover Stornetta Farms**
91 Lakeville Street
Petaluma, CA 94975
800-237-3315
www.cloverstornetta.com
*Organic and conventional milk, cheese, butter, yogurt, and sour cream, sold in grocery chain markets throughout California, Nevada, and Arizona.*

**DaVero Sonoma**
766 Westside Road (farm stand)
Healdsburg, CA 95448
888-431-8008
www.davero.com
*Olive oils, vinegars, jams, herbs, and wines, available by mail order and at the farm stand, the Healdsburg, Santa Rosa (Saturday), and Marin farmers' markets.*

**Della Fattoria Bakery & Cafe**
141 Petaluma Boulevard North
Petaluma, CA 94952
707-763-0161
www.dellafattoria.com
*Artisanal breads, cakes, and pastries. Lunch daily except Mondays; early dinner on Fridays. Goods are available in selected Northern California restaurants, gourmet food stores and farmers' markets; check web site for locations.*

**Dry Creek Peach & Produce**
2179 Yoakim Bridge Road
Healdsburg, CA 95448
707-433-8121
www.drycreekpeach.com
*Peaches, nectarines, plums, tomatoes, and Walla Walla onions, sold at the farm on Saturdays and Sundays, noon to 5 p.m., in July and August. Peaches are sold online, for July and August delivery within the continental United States and Hawaii. Most produce is also sold at Sonoma County farmers' markets, and at select gourmet food stores in the Northern California Bay Area, including Mollie Stone's and Whole Foods.*

**Eastside Farm** (Jeff and Susan Mall)
10900 Eastside Road
Healdsburg, CA 95448
707-953-1040
www.eastsidefarm.com
*Eggs, heirloom tomatoes, beans, squash, peppers, herbs, apples, pears, plums, nectarines, straw-berries, and blackberries, sold at Sonoma County farmers' markets. No retail sales at this location.*

**Fulton Valley Farms**
1200 River Road
P.O. Box 2
Fulton, CA 95439
707-546-8482
www.fultonvalley.com
*Range, roaster, organic, and halal chickens, sold at gourmet food stores and some chain markets in Northern California. No retail sales at this location.*

**Gourmet Mushrooms**
2901 Gravenstein Highway
Sebastopol, CA 95473
707-823-1743
www.gourmetmushroomsinc.com
*Exotic edible mushrooms and nutraceutical mushroom products, sold nationwide under the MYCOPIA brand at Whole Foods and other gourmet food stores. No retail sales at this location.*

**Hector's Honey Farm**
2794 Fulton Road
Fulton, CA 95439
707-579-9416
*Honey, honeycomb, beeswax candles, bee pollen, Araucana eggs, and tomatillos, sold at Sonoma County farmers' markets and at the farm, by appointment only.*

**Hobbs' Applewood Smoked Meat Company**
3701 Collins Avenue, Ste. 5C
Richmond, CA 94806
510-232-5577
*Bacon, prosciutto, corned beef, sausages, pork tenderloin, turkey, and other smoked meats sold at gourmet food stores in California. Bryan's Quality Meats in San Francisco sells and ships Hobbs' bacon nationwide. No retail sales at this location.*

Order from:
Bryan's Quality Meats
3473 California Street
San Francisco, CA 94118
415-752-0179

**Laura Chenel's Chèvre**
4310 Fremont Drive
Sonoma, CA 95476
707-996-4477
www.laurachenel.com
*Goat's milk cheeses, sold nationally at gourmet food stores and many supermarkets. No retail sales at this location.*

**Marshall's Farm**
159 Lombard Road
American Canyon, CA 94503
800-624-4637
www.marshallshoney.com
*Natural and organic honeys, beeswax, and beeswax candles, sold at the farm Mondays through Fridays, 10 a.m. to 5 p.m., at farmers' markets in Napa, Marin, San Francisco, and Oakland, and by mail order.*

**Nana Mae's Organics**
708 Gravenstein Highway North, No. 174
Sebastopol, CA 95472
707-829-7359
www.nanamae.com
*Organic apple ciders, juices, vinegars and sauces, pear juice, and honey, sold at the farm (by appointment only) July through December, and at gourmet grocery stores in Northern California.*

**Ridgecut Gristmills**
317 Fifth Street
P.O. Box 862
Arbuckle, CA 95912
530-476-3576
www.ridgecut.com
*Stone-ground cornmeal, cracked corn, corn bread mixes, and buckwheat butter-milk pancake mix, sold by mail order and at the Davis (CA) Food Co-op, the Nugget Markets chain in Northern California, and at Napa Valley farmers' markets.*

**Scharffen Berger Chocolate Maker**
www.scharffenberger.com
*Dark and milk baking chocolates, bars, nibs, and ganache. Sold nationally in most gourmet food stores and supermarkets.*

**Soda Rock Farm**
Healdsburg, CA 95448
707-433-4589
*Heirloom tomatoes and vegetables, sold at local farmers' markets and Big John's Market in Healdsburg. No retail sales at this location.*

**Sonoma County Poultry**
P.O. Box 140
Penngrove, CA 94951
800-953-8257
www.libertyducks.com
*Liberty Ducks, sold only to restaurants and by mail order.*

**Sparrow Lane**
P.O. Box 642
Keyes, CA 95328
866-515-2477
www.sparrowlane.com
*Extra-virgin olive oil, flavored oils, and vinegars, sold at West Coast gourmet markets and by mail order.*

**Terra Sonoma**
P.O. Box 444
Geyserville, CA 95441
707-431-1382
www.terrasonoma.com
*Verjus (unfermented grape juice), sold at Northern California gourmet food stores and by mail order. No retail sales at this location.*

**Tierra Vegetables Farm Stand**
651 Airport Boulevard at Highway 101
Santa Rosa, CA 95403
707-837-8366
www.tierravegetables.com
*Chiles, chile jams and powders, peppers, beans, pumpkins, squash, wool products, sold at the farm stand (days and hours vary by the season), Sonoma County farmers' markets, and select wine country gourmet food stores.*

**Zoe's Meats**
133 Copeland
Petaluma, CA 94952
707-763-9637
www.zoesmeats.com
*Prosciutto, salami, pancetta, mortadella, and other meats, available in restaurants and at gourmet food stores in California and Washington State, including Mollie Stone's. No retail sales at this location.*

**Rodney Strong Vineyards**
11455 Old Redwood Highway
Healdsburg, CA 95448
707-431-1533
www.rodneystrong.com
*Sonoma County wines, including Sauvignon Blanc, Chardonnay, Pinot Noir, Zinfandel, Syrah, Merlot, Cabernet Sauvignon, and the proprietary red wine Symmetry.*

## farmers' markets

**Cloverdale Certified Farmers' Market**
Cloverdale Boulevard between First and Second Streets: Fridays, June through September, 6:30 p.m. to 8:30 p.m.
707-894-9454

**Cotati Farmers' Market**
La Plaza Park, West Sierra and Old Redwood Highway: Thursdays, early June through early October, 4:30 p.m. to 7:30 p.m.
707-795-5508
www.cotati.org

**Guerneville Farmers' Market**
Guerneville Town Square: Wednesdays, 4 p.m. to 7 p.m., mid-May through late October

**Healdsburg Certified Farmers' Market**
Plaza and Center Streets: Tuesdays, 4 p.m. to 6:30 p.m., early June through late October
North and Vine Streets: Saturdays, 9 a.m. to noon, early May through late November
707-431-1956
www.healdsburgfarmersmarket.org

**Occidental Bohemian Farmers' Market**
Downtown Occidental: Fridays, 4 p.m. until dusk, June through October
707-793-2159
www.occidentalfarmersmarket.com

**Petaluma Farmers' Market**
Second Street between B & D Streets: Wednesdays, 4:30 p.m. to 8 p.m., mid-June to late August
Walnut Park, between Petaluma Boulevard South and D Street: Saturdays, 2 p.m. to 5 p.m.
707-762-0344
www.petalumafarmersmarket.com

**Santa Rosa Downtown Market**
Fourth Street from Mendocino Avenue to E Street: Wednesdays, 5 p.m. to 8:30 p.m., mid-May to mid-August
707-524-2123
www.srdowntownmarket.com

**Santa Rosa Original Farmers' Market**
Santa Rosa Veterans Building
1351 Maple Avenue: Wednesdays and Saturdays, 8:30 a.m. to noon, year-round
707-522-8629
santarosafarmersmarket.blogspot.com

**Sebastopol Farmers' Market**
Town Plaza at McKinley Street: Sundays, 10 a.m. to 1:30 p.m., April through November
707-522-9305

**Sonoma Farmers' Market**
Sonoma Plaza: Tuesdays, 5:30 p.m. until dusk, April through August.
Depot Park: Fridays, 9 a.m. to noon, year-round,
707-538-7023

**Windsor Certified Farmers' Market**
Windsor Town Green: Thursdays, 5 p.m. to 8 p.m., June through August; Sundays, 10 a.m. to 1 p.m., May through November
707-837-1320
www.windsorfarmersmarket.com

## organizations & events

**Gravenstein Apple Fair**
Ragle Ranch Park
500 Ragle Road
Sebastopol, CA 95472
707-824-1765
www.gravensteinapplefair.com
*An old-time country get-together held every August (usually the second weekend), with food booths, cooking demonstrations, apples, wine and beer tasting, and music.*

**Sonoma County Farm Trails**
P.O. Box 6032
Santa Rosa, CA 95406
707-571-8288 or 800-207-9464
www.farmtrails.org
*An association of 150 local farmers, ranchers, dairies, nurseries, wineries, and other producers who market their goods directly to consumers. Complimentary maps are available at Farm Trails member businesses and most Chambers of Commerce and visitor centers in the San Francisco North Bay area.*

**Sonoma County Vintners**
420 Aviation Boulevard, Suite 106
Santa Rosa, CA 95403
707-522-5840
www.sonomawine.com
*A marketing organization representing member Sonoma County wineries and grape growers.*

**Southern Foodways Alliance**
Center for the Study of Southern Culture
P.O. Box 1848
Barnard Observatory
University, MS 38677
662-915-5993
www.southernfoodways.com
*An organization committed to preserving traditional Southern foods, recipes, and cooking methods.*

**Slow Foods USA**
20 Jay Street, Ste. M04
Brooklyn, NY 11201
718-260-8000 or 877-SlowFood
www.slowfoodusa.org
*An organization dedicated to encouraging the production and consumption of sustainably raised, local foods.*

# index

143

# acknowledgments

**Jeff Mall:** Running a restaurant and putting together a cookbook require great teamwork. I could not have done this book without my team. First, I want to thank the best chef I know, my wife, Susan. Without her love and support, none of this would have happened. I want to give special thanks to my family for believing in me and to Scott Silva for being a lifelong friend and a great business partner. Many, many thanks go to the staff of Zin, both past and present. Your pride and hard work have made the restaurant what it is today. A million thanks to our best friends and partners in this project, Josh and Regina Silvers. And to Robert Larsen, Alan Campbell, Linda Murphy, Jennifer Barry, and the Klein family of Rodney Strong Vineyards—thank you for making the crazy idea that Josh and I had become a beautiful reality.

**Josh Silvers:** I would like to thank all the people who made *Down Home : Downtown* possible, especially my wife, Regina, without whom Syrah and this book would never have been. My thanks also go to Jeff and his wife, Susan, my friends and partners in this endeavor; to Robert Larsen, who made this book happen; and to Tom Klein and all the folks at Rodney Strong Vineyards. I am grateful to Alan Campbell, for his amazing photographs; to Linda Murphy, for translating my words into poetry; and to the best staff a chef could ever have. And finally, I want to thank book designer and packager Jennifer Barry, not just for putting up with me . . . but for putting it *all* together, better than I could have hoped for.